To Her

GIRL #85

A Doukhobor Childhood

Helen Chernoff Freeman

In Love
& Light
Helen Freeman

Produced by:

FriesenPress
Suite 300 – 852 Fort Street
Victoria, BC, Canada V8W 1H8

www.friesenpress.com

Distributed to the trade by The Ingram Book Company

Frightened and miles away from home,
Captured by tall chain link fencing.
Bleak, barren and frozen landscape or
Matrons, a comparable coldness
just the same.
Ever present ... white starched
inside and out ... no escape.
Harsh words, work and discipline only,
Never a hug for a hurt, or pure joy,
nor praise or any kindness.
I wanted to be loved.
I wanted Home.
So I wanted and I waited ... ...

HCF

Table Of Contents

Dedication

To my beautiful, precious children Chris and Nicole
and grandbaby Aubrie

Preface

This book began life as an attempt to help explain to my (now adult) children some of the things from my past they had grown up hearing about, but still understood imperfectly. As I worked on it, however, I came to realize that it had an audience well beyond my immediate family. Many friends in the Doukhobor community have expressed a keen interest in reading my recollections of an experience that touched us all. But beyond that, as I shared my story with my many friends and acquaintances in the wider community, their reaction tended to be one of amazement at a story they knew very little about, combined with an eagerness to learn more.

I was held at the New Denver School Dormitory from December 1955 until August 1959. My years spent there, which form the subject of this book, can only be described as a living hell. Revisiting those painful memories has not been easy. Nevertheless, my experience of life since leaving New Denver has taught me that a determination not to be crushed by the horrors of our past can be the first step towards true healing.

In presenting this very personal memoir to the public, it is my fervent hope that each and every reader, understanding what happened to the Freedomite children, would be inspired to intervene to stop the abuse of any child, no matter the circumstances. If so, my years in the New Denver School Dormitory will not have been entirely in vain.
May peace surround you.

Helen Chernoff Freeman
Agassiz, BC

Acknowledgements

My thanks are due to story editor Mark Brown and his wife Abigail, who together helped shape my many pages of recollections into a clear and forceful narrative - without sacrificing its emotional heart. Thanks also to Mark for preparing the photographs for reproduction and for designing the front cover artwork.

I would also like to thank former British Columbia Attorney General Geoff Plant for kindly giving me permission to reprint his letter to me.

But above all, the biggest thank you must go to my sisters Marie, Nina and late sister Kathrine, who lived this story with me.

Names in this account have been changed (apart from those of my immediate family), with the exception of Tad Mori. It is a privilege to honour by name a man of such deep humanity.

1. GRAND FORKS CHILDHOOD

September, 1955

Among the memories of my childhood I recall a sweltering day in late summer more than half a century ago. I was only a few weeks away from my eighth birthday, and was looking out the kitchen window of my parents' home in Grand Forks, a rural town in southern British Columbia just a few miles from the United States border.

Grandpa was weeding my mother's vegetable garden. I can still clearly see the trail of limp weeds on the parched earth behind him. My grandfather was a deeply religious man who believed in God, prayer, and the virtue of honest toil. He worked the way he prayed - slowly and deliberately, with a sense of being engaged in a task of the utmost importance. On the other side of the open window from me my grandmother was sitting on the back porch out of the fierce midday sun, shelling peas.

In the relative cool of the kitchen, my sister Kathrine and I were preparing a garlic sandwich for Grandpa. Kathrine was two years younger than me. Her task was to cut the freshly-picked, pungent green spikes to the right length, and mine was to carefully arrange them between slices of buttered, home-baked bread. If we made his sandwich well, we knew Grandpa might reward us with a handful of sun-warmed raspberries, and maybe a kiss. We loved raspberries, but shuddered at the thought of garlic kisses. Together we giggled, and teased Grandma over her inability to make garlic sandwiches just the way Grandpa liked them.

My mother was in the kitchen with us. Beets from the garden had been topped and tailed and set in a pot on the stove. That night, when it was cooler, Mother would make them into borscht following the recipe Grandma brought with her when she came to Canada from Tsarist Russia as a youngster in the late 1800s. Outside, my four-year-old sister Marie was playing with bugs in the dirt in her cotton dress and sun hat.

Grandpa took off his hat and wiped his forehead. "How long till lunch?" he called.

"Almost ready!" I replied.

He put his hoe aside and set up the sprinkler, then went over to turn on the water.

Suddenly Marie shrieked. Mother looked up, alarmed, but her concern turned to a smile as she saw my littlest sister scrambling to get out from under the cold jets of the sprinkler. After the initial shock, Marie became intrigued with the sprinkler's back-and-forth action, and followed it as closely as she dared, only to flee with squeals of delight each time it changed direction and threatened to drench her.

"Deda!" my mother called to Grandpa. "Lunch is ready now!"

"Edoo!" he called back, emerging from the vegetable garden and wiping the dirt from his hands.

Mother was about to call Marie, but instead she gasped. Little Marie was running through the sprinkler. My mother hurried outside to try and stop her. Marie took refuge under the sprinkler, laughing at her mother's efforts to catch her without getting soaked.

Suddenly a car was heard approaching. Grandpa stopped laughing, and looked toward the road. His eyes narrowed.

Mother tensed for an instant, then called Marie's name. Her voice had an edge to it that made the four-year-old freeze. My mother swooped through the sprinkler jets, snatched up my little sister, and ran with her back to the house. She thrust Marie into my arms, and told us to hide quickly. Without questioning her, the three of us ran for the trapdoor in the kitchen floor. We scrambled down into the cellar, shutting the door behind us. It was dark down there but for the faint light that came through a window level with the ground outside. As we fumbled our way in silence towards the crawl space under the house, car tires came to a stop right outside the cellar window.

Just then the trapdoor opened again. "Helen," my mother called as she threw a towel down to me, "dry your sister so she doesn't catch a chill!"

Kathrine squeezed into the crawl space while I hurriedly started drying Marie. She was frightened and unhappy, but knew not to complain out loud.

Outside, doors slammed and boots crunched on gravel. I finished drying Marie's hair. Footsteps sounded on the wooden porch, followed by a knock at the door. I quickly straightened Marie's still damp dress, and we both joined Kathrine in the crawl space, among the cobwebs and giant spiders.

Lying in the dark I heard my mother open the door, followed by the sound of men's voices, brusque and official. We shushed each other again, this time silently. It might be nothing, but we had to wait to be told it was safe to come out.

Then I heard heavy footsteps on the floorboards overhead, going from room to room. My stomach knotted in fear. Police!

It was me they were looking for. They came by unexpectedly, hoping to catch children who should have been in school. I knew if I were caught I'd be taken from my family and sent away. I was the only one of the three of us old enough; my sisters couldn't be removed from home because they were still under age, but Mom and Dad thought it best if none of us was sighted. We lay there in the cold and dark, listening to the footsteps of the police as they searched each room of our home. I held my breath, not daring to move a muscle, and prayed we wouldn't be found.

Suddenly, I froze.

The footsteps overhead had returned to the kitchen, and then stopped. I listened in terror as the trapdoor to the cellar creaked open. I could hardly breathe, I was so frightened. A police officer put his head in, and waved a flashlight around. Aware that this could be the last time I'd see my sisters, I put an arm around each of them. I prayed to make myself invisible as the flashlight swept the cellar. The beam picked out the darkened corners, the dirt floor, the jars filled with fruits and vegetables among all the empty crates and cartons awaiting the abundant harvest still growing in our garden.

The light was suddenly switched off. I realized the officer was listening for sounds of life. My heart was pounding so hard I was afraid he'd hear me. It was ages since I'd taken a breath. Finally he gave a grunt. "There's no one here." The trap door closed and the footsteps moved away. My whole body surged with relief.

The policemen left, after warning my mother they'd be back. I heard the car doors close and the crunch of tires on gravel. We waited in silence, long after the sound of the car had faded away. I felt light-headed, and realized I was still holding my breath. There was an air vent in the area, and we could crawl over to it on our hands and knees to make sure the coast was clear. I filled my lungs over and over with the warm, clean air from outside.

At last the trapdoor opened and my mother called us up, trying to hide the shaking in her voice. I leaped up the stairs three at a time, and threw myself into her arms. If I could only hug her tightly enough, I reasoned, nothing on earth could ever tear us apart.

* * *

My family were Doukhobors, a Christian sect that fled to Canada in the closing years of the nineteenth century to escape persecution in their home-land. Their uncompromising pacifism and distrust of any authority but that of their charismatic leaders had always made them difficult to govern. The last straw for Tsar Nicholas II came when thousands of Doukhobor conscripts had publicly burned their weapons rather than fight. It was a dramatic expression of Christian idealism that gained the admiration of many around the world, and made them enough of an embarrassment that the Tsar was only too glad to find another nation willing to take them off his hands.

The Canadian government in Ottawa had initially welcomed these peace-loving refugees from feudal autocracy, even going so far as to concede to their demand for exemption from military service. The arrangement seemed advantageous to both parties, as the Doukhobors were notoriously devoted to hard work and Canada at the turn of the century had vast tracts of land that needed to be brought under cultivation swiftly. However, the newcomers brought with them their traditional values, which didn't always sit well with those of the thriving, forward-looking society they found in the new country.

The first major obstacle came after just a few years, when the government reneged on the terms of the original land grants by demanding an oath of alle-giance before the Doukhobors could gain title to lands they'd already settled and improved. The community pointed out that it was against their religion to swear such oaths to a mere worldly authority. It was, in fact, one of the prime reasons Tsar Nicholas had found them such an irritation. The govern-ment stood firm, and many saw the land they'd worked revert to the Crown. A sizeable number of Doukhobors protested by stripping off their clothes and marching nude in public. The idea was to draw attention to their plight by asserting the inherent simple dignity of the human person. The government responded by putting offenders in jail.

Not all were dissatisfied though, and differences of opinion arose in the community about how best to live an authentic Doukhobor life in this new land that had adopted them. Fault lines appeared between those who wanted to maintain a way of life centred on their traditional religious beliefs and practices, and those who were prepared to submit to civil authority and accept the ways of the host country. The former gathered under the banner of the Christian Community of Universal Brotherhood; the latter became known as Independent Doukhobors. My mother's grandfather, Nicholas Zebroff, was among those who thought assimilation was dangerous. He organized a more radical splinter-group called the Sons of Freedom, made up of those who felt the Doukhobors were making too many concessions to the ways of Canadian society.

My father's parents, Mike and Helen Chernoff, became Independent Doukhobors. They chose to settle in Saskatchewan and adopted the ways of the rest of society. They took land and farmed it, and that's how my father was raised. As children we had little to do with them; I recall seeing them for the first time the year after I turned seven. I thought Grandma Chernoff was quite elegant. She had curly hair and wore English-style dresses, whereas my mother's mother only ever wore traditional Doukhobor dress. I was quite proud of my father's mother, and of his father too, who looked like a very proper English gentleman. My sisters and I were sorry we never really knew our paternal grandparents. My father had a brother, Michael, a sister Pauline, and another brother, who died in childhood. As a young man he lived an Independent Doukhobor lifestyle. He played in a band, smoked some, and even took the occasional drink.

Within a decade of emigrating to Canada, enough Doukhobors were chafing at what they perceived to be unnecessary government interference in their lives that a second exodus took place, this time further westward in the hope of finding a place where they could live out their motto of 'Toil and Peaceful Life' unmolested. The Christian Community of Universal Brotherhood bought land in British Columbia, and its members moved there, settling in Grand Forks and other areas. There they lived a communal lifestyle, in which everyone took turns doing different jobs. As time went on, their largest presence came to be in the Kootenays, a mountainous area of fertile valleys drained by the Kootenay and Columbia rivers in the southeasternmost corner of the province, nestled against the Rockies and the United States border.

My mother's parents, John and Anastasia Zebroff, were staunch Freedomites, as the Sons of Freedom became known, and came out to British Columbia to live as community Doukhobors. Grandpa worked in the orchards, pruning, weeding, and picking the fruit. Grandma Zebroff was always a housewife. They had six children. Only my mother, Mary, the youngest, and my aunt Annie, the oldest, survived to adulthood. Both Grandpa and Grandma lived an observant, communal lifestyle, never protesting or getting imprisoned, and that's how my mother was raised.

One important consequence of these repeated upheavals is that those who ended up in British Columbia tended to be more set in their ways than other Doukhobors, more suspicious of the civil authority, and more ready to go to extreme lengths to preserve their way of life. Due in part to this reluctance to compromise, internal dissension continued, triggered by resistance to the civil requirement to register vital statistics, seen as a prelude to conscription, to the individual registration of land, which threatened community life, and to compulsory public education. Many Freedomite parents refused to send their children to school on the grounds that they believed public education to be militaristic, and to teach exploitation of others. The government denied this, but the situation wasn't helped when, with the First World War looming, the Department of Education introduced military drills and rifle practice in schools. Once again, nude protests achieved nothing except the arrests of those involved.

The provincial government saw no need to cater to the Freedomites' concerns. When parents not sending their children to school ignored the fines imposed, the provincial government passed legislation holding the entire community responsible for the unpaid fines. Hotheads retaliated by burning down a Doukhobor-owned school. The confrontation escalated, and soon spread beyond just schools to include the burning of homes and businesses of other Doukhobors. From there the destruction continued out into the wider community, destroying public buildings, and even a bridge.

Caught in the middle, the Doukhobor leadership was helpless. The community built schools with their own money, and fanatics within that same community burned them down. Whenever anyone was arrested and charged with arson, mass demonstrations followed in which hundreds of Freedomites, men and women, would strip to the skin and march in public to protest the crass materialism that could imagine a wooden schoolhouse to be of more value than a Spirit-filled prophet proclaiming the gospel of salvation with a can of kerosene and a box of matches.

A split within the community was inevitable. The leadership wanted respectability and a peaceful coexistence with their neighbours, and saw no need to antagonize the government. So when Freedomites came out of prison after being arrested for protesting nude they now found themselves shunned by the community. Many gravitated to the ramshackle village of Krestova in the arid Crescent Valley area, which soon found itself an unofficial centre of Freedomite activity. The Christian Community of Universal Brotherhood eventually went bankrupt due to a combination of economic factors and loss of members. It was replaced by another organization, but the communal life would never return in the same way.

* * *

This was the situation my father encountered when he came to Grand Forks from Kylemore, Saskatchewan as a young man in the 1940s. His primary purpose in visiting was to see his Aunt Mabel Arishenkoff who lived there, but while he was in town he also met my mother.

My father, John Chernoff, was a real giant of a man. He was handsome, with broad, powerful shoulders and the most beautiful blue eyes. He was very soft-spoken, but with a strong, deep singing voice. My mother, Mary Zebroff, had brown hair and bright brown eyes. She too had a soft voice, and, like my father, was also a beautiful singer. As smoking, drinking and dancing were not tolerated by Freedomites, there was doubtless some concern about this sharp-dressed, worldly young Independent from the Prairies courting the grand-daughter of the founder of the Freedomites. Nevertheless, my parents married in December 1946, when my dad was twenty-four and my mom twenty-one. I was born nine months later, on September 22, 1947, in Oliver, a fruit-picking area at the southernmost end of British Columbia's fertile Okanagan Valley. I had brown eyes like my mom, and was given the name Helen after my father's mother.

Two years later I got a little sister, Kathrine, and was delighted I now had a real live doll of my own to play with. Kathrine was beautiful, with Dad's sandy-coloured hair and his same, intense blue eyes. Eighteen months later another sister, Marie, came along. She too had Dad's sparkling blue eyes. As she grew, her hair became the colour of freshly-fallen snow.

For a time, my father worked in the coal mine in Greenwood. Later, he worked unloading coal from the trains onto a truck for distribution to the people of Grand Forks. By the time I turned eight he'd been working as a logger for a while. Sometimes he'd be home every night, but other times the work took him off into the bush for days at a stretch. It was tiring work, and he'd come home exhausted, wanting quiet so he could read and unwind. We'd try and be on our best behaviour for him, but it wasn't easy, as we were lively, fun-loving children. He was strict, and could yell or give us a spanking just as soon as look at us. Sometimes he grew a beard, and then he really looked terrifying.

When he wasn't yelling at us though, his voice could be so soft we'd have to put our ears almost to his mouth to hear what he was saying. And if he was wearing his reading glasses at the time, we thought he looked like a professor. He sounded like one too, as he was extremely well-read. I'd listen in on some of his conversations with other adults and stare in amazement at his choice of words. I'd look up the words later, and through that became quite good at using the dictionary and at learning to spell.

Mom stayed at home, and was always there when we needed her. Our family was neither rich nor dirt poor, though there were days when I used to wonder why I couldn't have a new toy or a new pair of shoes, when others (or so I imagined) got them any time their hearts desired. Since we grew up at just above poverty level, Mom rarely purchased anything new to wear. Instead, she made most of her clothes, and almost all of ours, herself. She was an extremely hard-working woman, whose chores seemed never to be over. As the three of us lay in bed, tucked in for the night, we'd hear her still ironing or baking. My sisters and I agreed that our mother was the kindest, most gener-ous, most spiritual, most beautiful woman on the face of the earth. She loved her girls beyond reason, and no task was too much if it concerned us and our well-being. She was gentle and affectionate, and could be very funny, too. Not many children our age got to laugh with their mothers the way we did.

As we children grew, we enjoyed each other's company. Kathrine considered herself a princess, and certainly liked to look the part. She always had the extra ruffles on her dress and the most ribbons in her hair. She didn't like to get dirty, and whenever we made mud pies she'd be washing her hands continually. Marie, on the other hand, was fearless in everything. She wore ragged jeans, and shirts that seemed either too big or too small. She was a tough little girl, but would share anything that was hers. I loved to hold her and cuddle her, because in my world she was my doll number two.

Because he was away working so much, we valued what time we had with our father. He loved to play the guitar, and my sisters and I loved to sing along with him. When Mom accompanied Dad they both sang so beautifully we three girls just sat and stared. We thought they should be on the stage, and that we sounded like frogs compared to them.

When he'd married, Dad had adopted the traditions of his Freedomite bride's family, with the exception of their prohibition on dancing. He no longer danced, and Mom certainly never did, but he didn't stop us when we got the urge. When I was six, 'This Ole House' by Rosemary Clooney was at number one in the charts. My sisters and I loved to roll up the rug and dance to it, singing at the top of our lungs, while Dad's six strings laid down a beat that bounced off the walls and made the floorboards ring. This, of course, never happened when our grandparents were around, as they thought dancing was evil.

Our mother's elder sister Anne owned and ran a small corner store with her husband, Uncle Mike, less than a block away. Auntie Vatkin, as we called her, was taller than our mother, and skinny compared to most women we knew. When she was young she'd worked in the apple orchards, carrying ladders from tree to tree. Her hands were swollen with arthritis from as far back as I can remember, and yet she worked, and worked hard, all the time. Auntie Vatkin was some sixteen years older than my mother, and never had children of her own. So from my birth onwards she decided to take charge of her younger sister's children, and as we grew the three of us became as if we were hers.

My sisters and I always looked on our aunt as a trailblazer. There were not many women in business in those days, certainly not Doukhobor, and especially not Freedomite. She wore pants most of the time, something very few Doukhobor women did back then, and her hair was cut quite short and permed. A neighbour did the perm, and I loved going along to watch. My auntie also drove a late-40s or early-50s stick-shift Austin that looked like it had a hunchback. Hardly any women drove in those days, and it was fun to go cruising with her. Sometimes she'd drive out to Christina Lake, about ten miles from Grand Forks, and let us wade in the water up to our knees.

We loved going round to her store. She made the biggest ice cream cones, with several scoops of different flavours piled so high we feared they'd topple. Kathrine got to pick her treat first, because she was younger than me. I never minded, because there was always plenty to choose from. Away from the store our auntie snuck candies to us when our mom had her back turned. Needless to say, we loved her to pieces. She had a great sense of humour, and we loved helping out in her store just so we could enjoy her company. She was like a mom, but she was also our best friend. Our dad was busy a lot of the time, and our mom didn't care for some of our shenanigans, but Auntie Vatkin was always game for whatever scheme we came up with.

My mother's parents lived further up the hill, about an hour's walk from our house, and we saw them almost on a daily basis. Grandpa Zebroff was tall, very dark-skinned from a lifetime of working in the open air, and had a full beard and moustache. Grandma Zebroff was shorter, very pretty, and fairly slim. Her long hair was woven into a silver braid and tied in a bun at the nape of her neck. She'd had cataracts removed from both eyes, and wore thick glasses which were so heavy she tied a shoe lace around the arms to keep them from falling off. Her clothing was always in the traditional Doukhobor style; a long skirt, a long-sleeved blouse, and the ever-present apron. She also wore a scarf all the time – kerchief would better describe it – folded into a triangle and tied in a knot under the chin.

Because our grandparents were so religious, a lot of our time with them was spent learning lengthy hymns, prayers and other devotions, which we were then expected to recite by heart. To ensure our fullest co-operation, they'd make a contest of it. On the wall in their house hung a cabinet that held the few dishes they owned, along with a big bowl that was always filled with the most delicious candy. The side of the cabinet holding the candy was kept locked, and we'd scream with delight when Grandma reached for the key. We knew that whoever could learn a new prayer the fastest would get the biggest piece of candy.

Our grandparents' home was small and simple. The walls were adorned with pages taken from Eaton's catalogues and Maclean's and Life magazines. The pages formed a crust several layers thick, since Grandma would redo them every few years as the colours faded. She'd whitewash over the old pages, then stick the new pages on with flour paste while the walls were still damp. Whenever we visited we'd spend hours looking at old pictures of once-new fashions, or read about interesting people in distant parts of the world, or marvel at exotic and improbable plants and animals, all plastered on the walls of our grandparents' place.

They had no television, no radio, no electricity, and none of the modern conveniences most people took for granted. Their only book was a Russian Bible. Yet every time we visited we felt we were on an adventure. As we walked the hillsides, Grandpa taught us about different plants, what berries were edible, what wild animals might be lurking nearby. It was all done in Russian; he refused to speak to us in English, first of all because Grandma wouldn't understand, and secondly, and more importantly, he'd say, so we didn't forget our language, our heritage and our culture.

Most mornings Grandpa would walk down the hillside and be weeding in the garden before we were even awake. Grandma often came with him, and while he was in the garden she'd be in the kitchen preparing breakfast. With the smells of warm porridge cooking and fresh home-made bread being toasted, it wasn't hard to jump out of bed and greet the day with a smile on my face.

There were a few Freedomite families in Grand Forks, and these folks came by on a regular basis. We girls were always happy to see guests, especially if they had children. Dad's Aunt Mabel still lived in Grand Forks, a short walk away from us, and we'd often stroll over for a cup of tea on a Saturday afternoon.

We had a lot of company from the Doukhobor areas of the Kootenays. When Freedomites travelled from there to the coast our home was a natural stopping place for them. Sometimes they'd just visit for coffee or lunch, but often people would stay overnight. Members of different choirs would stop in as well. Other than that, we pretty much kept to ourselves.

This then was my everyday existence. I was raised in a happy, loving family home where prayer and moral integrity were valued, and where we were surrounded by music, laughter, and many, many hugs and kisses. There were storm clouds gathering on the horizon though, and our quiet world was about to be shattered in a huge, awful and heartbreaking way.

* * *

The discontent simmering among some of the Freedomites of British Columbia had never gone away. Destruction of property had continued in the Kootenays, with an ongoing spate of bombings and arson throughout the 1940s. During this time the region was as if in a state of siege, with Independent and Orthodox Doukhobors as well as public bodies having to post guards on their properties night and day to prevent their destruction. In spite of these precautions losses mounted, and people continued to live in fear of losing their livelihoods.

Not all Doukhobors rejected public education. In fact, when a proposal by the leadership to build private Doukhobor schools was turned down by the provincial authorities, the mainstream Doukhobor community reluctantly accepted public schooling, with provision for Russian language classes and other cultural activities outside of regular school hours. Only Freedomite parents kept their children away, maintaining that public schools were still nurseries of militarism and capitalism. Arrests were followed by nude demonstrations, followed in turn by more arrests.

British Columbia governments had wrestled for decades with the problem of how to deal with the Freedomites' tendency to flaunt civil authority. Reports and inquiries had been commissioned, but no end was in sight. They were frustrated. They had hoped to 'Canadianize' Freedomite children through the public school system, but that couldn't happen if parents were keeping their children away from school out of fear of that very indoctrination.

Determined to resolve the issue once and for all, the British Columbia government made the decision to take Freedomite children not attending school away from the influence of their families, in an attempt to prevent the spread of lawlessness to the next generation. The government's child welfare officers urged caution, but to the government of the day it was the only option that seemed to hold out any hope of bringing lasting peace to the Kootenays. So in 1953 the government had a former tuberculosis sanatorium in the small interior town of New Denver prepared to receive the children of recalcitrant Freedomites. And then they began looking for the truants with which they hoped to fill it.

It didn't take long. At the start of the new school year police broke up a nude protest by Freedomites in the small community of Perry Siding. The adults were sent to Vancouver for trial and sentencing, and their children became the first inmates of the New Denver sanatorium in its new role. Other children were seized by police and child welfare officers over the following months, on the grounds that their parents weren't sending them to school. Then January 1955 brought reports of a dawn raid by police in Krestova in which forty children just waking up were torn from their mothers' arms and taken to New Denver. And still the police looked for more.

Before long the mere mention of New Denver struck fear into any Freedomite heart. Parents visiting their children brought back reports of the terrible conditions there; the cold, the bad food, the lack of care by staff. By the middle of 1955 the number of children in the New Denver dormitory had risen to over seventy, and the Freedomites had protested their abduction in a telegram to the United Nations. While my sisters and I were hiding in our parents' cellar, a delegation of parents was vainly pleading in a Nelson court-room for the return of their children. They also appealed to British Columbia premier W.A.C. Bennett, but there was no sympathy there - the government's response was that the children would go home only when their parents agreed to send them to public school.

We heard about all this, and knew the police would continue looking for me too. It wasn't entirely clear to me why we were being hunted down. I knew the reason given was that we weren't going to school, but that didn't seem enough to tear us away from our families.

I knew my parents' stand was a principled one, but looking back I can only guess at their motives. The first half of the twentieth century had already seen two world wars, culminating in the explosion of two atomic bombs, each of which had destroyed a city in the blink of an eye. Instead of shrinking back in horror from such an evil, the world's powers seemed actually to be contemplating a future in which this would be an accepted way of resolving differences between nations. The British Columbia Ministry of Education didn't seem to be doing much shrinking back either. In fact, it seemed quite comfortable with the idea, so long as the right side came out on top. Since my parents believed nuclear warfare was an abomination, it would make sense to them that people who advocated it shouldn't be entrusted with the teaching of little children.

That much would have been clear in 1953, when the provincial government had started removing children from their parents. At the time my story begins it was 1955. In January of that year, the United States had announced its plan to place missiles armed with nuclear warheads in Western Europe, aimed at the Soviet Union. Largely in response to that, the eight-nation Warsaw Pact was quickly established, declaring that an attack on one member would be taken as an attack on all. Both sides were shaping up for a nuclear showdown that threatened unimaginable casualties, yet the two opposing camps dared not back down. Instead, the stakes were being raised higher and higher. No one knew for certain how far it could go, but even the very real possibility of annihilation of the greater part of humanity didn't seem to stop them. Actually consenting to allow their children's values to be shaped by followers of such a criminally reckless philosophy could surely never have been considered a serious option by my parents.

But if this was their line of thought, I knew nothing of it at the time. I was a mere child of eight, much too young to comprehend what was going on. The only thing that mattered to me was that my sisters and I were safe, never hungry, and had all the love our hearts could ever want.

2. TAKEN AWAY!

December, 1955

Our home stood on a corner lot on the outskirts of an area known as West Grand Forks. To the west and north of the house lay the huge vegetable garden, while to the south were various outbuildings, including a woodshed, an old bathhouse that my sisters and I used to play in, a small attached shed that housed our dad's tools, and the outdoor toilet. In front of these buildings rose a large grape arbour on which were grown huge, succulent purple grapes, small juicy green clusters, and two-toned varieties that tasted better than candy. The land further west of us was given over to potatoes, acres of which were grown there year after year.

The house itself was not large, having just two bedrooms, a kitchen, a front living room and a dining room. The front room was furnished with an old burgundy chesterfield and chair, each covered with a green throw. There were a couple of end tables built by my father, and lamps, which he fashioned out of large apple juice cans. In the back bedroom shared by my sisters and I were small three-drawer dressers also made by our dad. We had two beds topped with home-made mattresses, which swallowed us up when we leaped onto them.

All summer long our doors and windows were flung wide open against the sweltering heat, but in winter the back bedroom became so cold it was closed off, and the dining room was turned into a temporary bedroom for us children. There was no door, so we had to run into the attached storage room when we needed to change. The kitchen too was cold at that time of year if we moved any distance away from the old wood-burning range, and the windows had frost on them all the time. My sisters and I would huddle over breakfast as the pale sun struggled to get through the frost-encased pane, daring each other to lick the glass to see if our tongue would stick. Whenever it did, a fleeting panic would seize us, until the glass warmed enough and we were free.

Outside, the snow piled up until we could walk on top of it, listening to it crunch under our feet as we made our way to our auntie's store. The train station was almost visible from our house, and the eerie sound of a whistle blowing after dark, when the moon was full and the shadows danced around us, could make our hair stand on end. It was a time when everything seemed to be frozen, waiting to be released by the breath of an impossibly distant spring.

The first Thursday of December 1955 was bitterly cold, as it had been all week. My mother was busy as usual with housework, having taught us our lessons earlier. Mom was Freedomite to the very core of her being, so she wasn't about to send us to public school. But neither did she want her children growing up illiterate. Her solution was to see to our education herself, even though that too was against the law at the time.

Our home schooling had started very early, before we were even aware of it. Most Doukhobors only spoke Russian, but my parents had brought us up speaking both English and Russian. Formal teaching started early as well, though there was no set schedule for classes. The most convenient time tended to be while Mom did the ironing. As Mom ironed, one of us would ask a question about something that was important to us, and she'd take time to answer. There'd be answers for all the whys and whens we could possibly come up with. She answered questions about Communism, or Queen Elizabeth, or the Catholic Church, always being careful to let us think for ourselves. She had only a grade four education, so I was astounded at her range of knowledge.

After teaching me to read and write, she'd put questions on a piece of paper and I'd pretend to be in school, as would my two sisters. Because she made a game of it, we were always eager to learn more. Then she'd throw out random pieces of information that would stick in my mind, eventually stimulating further inquiry. Mom was very patient with us, teaching so gently we didn't even realize we were being taught. As a result, by the age of eight I not only spoke English well, but I read it and wrote it beautifully too. I was also making good progress in arithmetic, and had a great interest in history and geography.

That afternoon Mom was folding laundry prior to stacking firewood, as Dad was off working in the woods and wouldn't be home until later. Kathrine,

Marie and I were playing happily, cut-out paper dolls scattered over the living room floor.

The knock at the door was very quiet. Mom answered it, thinking it was one of the neighbours. When she said hello, we sisters ran into the kitchen to see who'd come to visit. Two men in suits and ties stood there. At first Mom thought they were salesmen, but when they identified themselves her face drained of colour. Mom's words were so soft we couldn't hear what was being said. Even so, my heart almost stopped. It was the police. I knew it without a doubt.

No one had heard the car pull up. They'd come quietly, and were in the kitchen before any of us realized what was happening. I wanted to bolt out the door, and run somewhere, anywhere, just please God don't let them take me to that awful place.

"Not just yet," I heard my mother plead. "We have to get her ready." She needed a little time, she said, to pack my clothes and make sure I had a bath, say a few prayers, and to let me say goodbye to my sisters and grandparents and aunt. She asked the two men if it would be all right if they left for a short while and then came back for me.

There was silence, then earnest whispering.

"Two hours," they said. "And she'd better be here waiting!"

I watched in amazement as the two men respectfully tipped their hats to my mother, then turned and left.

Without me!

I jumped for joy! They hadn't taken me away!

I ran to my mother. "Thank you, Mom! You saved me!"

My mother hugged me. She was sobbing softly. "Helen," she said, "they'll be back. They're giving us a couple of hours so I can bathe you, and braid your beautiful long, golden brown hair."

"But I can hide! They'll never find me!"

Tears ran down my mother's face. "I've given my word, Helen, and I intend to keep it."

I was stunned. Mom held me close as she stroked my hair. "In my heart I want to run with you, Helen. I want to hide you from that terrible place. But I gave my word that you'd still be here when they come for you."

Deep, wrenching sobs took hold of me. I didn't understand about giving your word. All I felt was confusion and fear, even betrayal. How could my mother just give me away like a used piece of clothing? I was far too young to understand what true belief is; what it is to be prepared even to let your child be taken away, because you believe in something so much more powerfully, as she did.

"But I don't want to go!" I wept uncontrollably. I loved my family and our home. My little sisters joined me in a chorus of sobbing and wailing. And yet, despite her tears, my mother remained calm. She directed Kathrine to run to Auntie Vatkin's store.

"Tell her what's happened. Ask her to drive to Deda and Baba's and bring them here. We have to say prayers for Helen's safe journey, and make our goodbyes."

My sister was off and running.

"And be quick! There isn't much time!"

* * *

Mom got the big old galvanized tub from the porch. She filled the tub with hot water and soap suds, and I sank in. She took the ribbons from my hair, gently undid my braids, then washed me, as if for the last time. Her tears fell in the tub, but when I looked up she smiled and pretended all was well.

My sister burst in, breathless, and said that Auntie had left at once for our grandparents' house and they'd all be here in a matter of minutes.

My world was coming to an end. I'd heard the stories about New Denver, and now I was being prepared to go there. Kathrine and Marie were running around, hollering, wanting to know if they too were going with me. I was trying to focus on what was happening, but my mind was spinning. How would I live without my family? Who'd braid my hair, kiss my hurts away, tuck me into bed at night? Would anyone play hide-and-seek with me? Would I ever see my sisters again?

When the bath was over, Mom dried me, but her tears kept leaving little streaks down my neck and back. She lovingly braided my long brown hair again. "Nice and tight," she said to herself, quietly and sadly. Then she dressed me in an outfit she'd made herself. "I'm not sure how long the trip will take, and I want you to look your best."

While she was still dressing me, Deda and Baba and Auntie Vatkin arrived.

"Oh my! Oh my God! What's to happen to all of us!"

"Our little Onnycheechka!"

"How we love you!"

"And how we're going to miss you!"

My grandparents immediately fell to their knees. "We must pray! For Helen, and for all of us!"

We all joined in. "Lord, help us to get through this ordeal."

"Let all be well."

"May the journey be a safe one."

We prayed together, asking God for guidance and protection. We went through every prayer we knew, and then said them all over again.

The emotions running through me were indescribable. Fear was uppermost. But at the same time, the idea of meeting a group of children like myself excited me.

"Mama, Baba, Auntie! Don't cry! Please don't cry! Can't you see I'm going on a journey?"

Since I knew very few Freedomite girls in Grand Forks, the prospect of this journey made my eight-year-old mind reel with anticipation. But I also had questions.

"Why am I being sent away to school when I study lessons at home already?"

No one could answer that.

One other question remained unspoken, but tore at my heart. How could my parents ever let me go?

Mom had packed a little brown suitcase for me. I noticed that Dad had engraved my initials on the front. HJCH. Helen J. (after my father) Chernoff. I was pleased. No one would dare steal it. We prayed more, and then more. I remember at one point the family crowded onto the couch, and photos were taken. And then, amid all the chaos, my father arrived home from work.

No words were necessary. He saw Grandpa on his knees in prayer. He saw my mother, her eyes red from weeping. And he saw my little brown suitcase by the door. He stood in stunned silence. He'd always known that one day they'd come for me, but no doubt clung to the faint hope that somehow I'd be overlooked. He came over to me and hugged me without speaking, and together we all sang the Lord's Prayer. The feeling in the room was as though someone had died.

After we'd prayed, everyone became animated again, giving me instructions on how to behave, how to braid my hair properly, how to talk to people, how to eat. Mom was frantic, trying to remember everything she meant to tell me before I left. "Write often. Wear warm clothes. Cover your head in winter. Don't try to run away. Remember, we love you!"

Dad reminded me to be obedient. "Always listen, and do as you're told. Don't argue, especially with your caregivers. Remember to call them 'Auntie'; it's respectful."

Grandma and Grandpa and Auntie added to the confusion.

"Learn as best you can."

"Please, just be a good little girl!"

"Don't forget how much we all love you."

"Many hugs and kisses!"

And then Auntie, who'd been looking out the window every two or three minutes, said, "They're back!"

We all heard the car on the gravel, and fell silent. I feared I might throw up. Then we heard the knock on the door. They'd returned. The same two who'd been there earlier. My mother had kept her promise, and they'd kept theirs.

One last, desperate thought struck me. "What if they aren't police? Did you check to see who they really are, Mom? What if I'm being kidnapped?"

"Come now, Helen."

I suddenly started sobbing again. Around me were the ones I loved most in the world. Dad, trying to be strong. My sisters, holding my hands as if my life was slipping away. Deda and Baba holding on to each other. Auntie wringing her arthritic hands. And, closest to me, my mother, her arms around me. A soft knock on the door, and it was time for me to leave them all behind. I said a silent prayer. *Please Lord, keep me safe!*

I picked up my suitcase. Mom led me out, with the rest of the family close behind. One of the men took my case and put it on the back seat. I climbed in, and the door closed behind me. I couldn't believe what was happening. I had no idea how long it would be before I'd return home again. Through the window I saw my family standing, watching me leave, tears flowing down their cheeks.

The car started to move. Now, even with the anticipation of meeting new friends, I was terrified. Dad was holding Mom because she looked as if she were about to collapse. My sisters waved slowly and sadly, bewilderment on their faces. Deda and Baba were inconsolable. My auntie was trying to keep up to the slowly moving car. And I was sitting in the back seat, waving to them all. This picture of my family remains etched in my mind. I am crying, and the two men are trying to comfort me. I am still looking back, back at my family, my life. I wave until they disappear, as we round the corner past my auntie's store.

* * *

The two men and I were about to travel from Grand Forks to New Denver. I knew it would be a very long journey. New Denver lay on the east shore of Slocan Lake in the Selkirk Mountains, and to get there we'd be going through the heart of Doukhobor country. It was late afternoon when we left, in the dead of winter, and we had to go over a mountain pass. There was a lot of snow. The idea was too frightening to comprehend.

My heart was aching for my family already and we'd barely left town. Yet I felt vaguely exhilarated too, for I sensed the adventure in the making. I could write to my family as often as I wanted, because I was sure there'd be lots to tell. I knew nothing about New Denver really, except that it wasn't a nice place to go. What would I eat there? What kind of clothing would I have to wear? Prison issue, presumably. I felt like a criminal although I'd done nothing wrong.

There was little conversation between the two men and me. They asked few questions, and I answered in fewer words. I thought instead about what I'd do when I got to New Denver; how I'd act, telling myself over and over that all would be well. I tried to remember my parents' instructions: be kind, be polite, be neat, be friendly, and above all, remember to be respectful to the caregivers. Don't try to run away, wear your mitts and galoshes and coat, don't argue with anyone, be a good girl. But most of all, remember how much we love you.

At that particular moment I didn't feel very loved. I felt very alone.

The rest of my thoughts were hazy. The men hadn't asked, and I hadn't told them, that I could get horribly sick while travelling. Whenever I travelled with my Auntie Vatkin she let me sit in the front passenger seat, and opened the window to let in fresh air if I started to feel ill. The men made me sit in the back, and kept the window tightly closed against the cold. While sickly fumes from the dashboard heater swirled around my head the men smoked, and the combined smells of tobacco smoke and warm engine oil made me nauseous. The sliding of the car through the slush and snow made it worse. Before we got as far as Christina Lake I was carsick.

We stopped at a diner and I went in and cleaned myself up. We did this the first few times, but the men soon realized we'd be on the road for a week if they stopped each time I threw up. I found some comfort if I pulled my jacket over my head and inhaled, and the familiar smell of home surrounded me. But this lasted only a few minutes, and then the waves of nausea returned. I threw up again and again, until I felt my insides were in the plastic bag they gave me. I wasn't a big girl, and I wondered if there'd be any of me left by the time we got to New Denver.

After a while we stopped at a restaurant. The two men offered to take me in for a bite to eat.

"No thanks," I groaned.

"Don't be stupid, kid! Come on!"

"But I just can't! It hurts too much."

They locked the doors, and told me to stay while they went inside. I was in the back seat, sick, frightened and alone. I was able to rest, because the car wasn't moving and the nausea receded. I stank from the vomit in my hair and on my clothes.

There was no heat in the car with the engine off. It was bitterly cold, and I was afraid I'd be frozen to death by the time they got back. What was keeping them? I had no idea where we were. Any thoughts of running from the car were quashed when I remembered what my mom had told me. I didn't want to die in the middle of nowhere, all by myself. I curled up on the seat and tried unsuccessfully to sleep.

I was shivering when the two men finally returned. They had alcohol on their breath. I hated that smell. It reminded me of Auntie Vatkin's husband, Uncle Mike. I used to feed him raw eggs and crackers when he'd been drinking. He talked funny and didn't make much sense when he was full of liquor. We started to move. While the men made jokes and laughed, I pretended I was asleep. Travelling the winding roads made me throw up all over again. My clothes were covered, and the men were not amused. The car smelled awful.

Whenever my Auntie Vatkin would drive us to our grandparent's home way up on the hill I used to think we'd fall off the road as we slowly, and I mean slowly, crawled up their very steep, narrow driveway. I'd be frozen with fear, whimpering like a wounded dog, while my aunt laughed all the way. The roads I travelled with the two men that night were steeper, the curves tighter, and we took them faster than even my auntie would have dared. We drove through the darkness on ice and snow, inches away from precipitous drops, for what seemed a lifetime. The car slid every now and then, and I was terrified. The sound of the men talking made my head spin. I wrapped my head into my coat once again, and eventually succeeded in falling asleep.

I woke just as dawn was breaking. There was a lake to the left of the road that was calm, and unbelievably beautiful.

"Hey kid," one of the men said, "that's the place up ahead."

I looked where he was pointing, and could just make out the dim outline of a large building down beside the lake. My stomach churned, wondering what awaited me in such a gloomy and forbidding place. I envisioned torture chambers underground. I feared it was not going to be a nice place to live.

The car stopped at a guard shack at the entrance to the property. The driver wound down the window and cold, fresh air spilled into the car. A shadowy figure asked why we were there.

"RCMP," the driver said. "Delivering a kid."

"What's the name?"

"Chernoff."

The guard checked his clipboard by the light spilling from the small shack behind him.

"Who?"

"Helen Chernoff. From Grand Forks."

"You just drove from there?"

"Sure did."

The guard gave a low whistle. He was having difficulty finding my name. I experienced a final, desperate hope that it wouldn't be there, that they wouldn't take me, that the two men would have to drive me back again! I would gladly have endured another drive back over the mountains if it meant I could be home with my loving family, far from that place.

The guard found my name, and grunted approval. "Okay. Go ahead."

My heart sank. They were expecting me. The driver wound the window back up, and we drove up to the front door.

3. BECOMING GIRL #85

December, 1955

The car stopped in a open space between two long, low wooden buildings, and we got out. I was covered in vomit, my joints were stiff from the trip and my face was green, but I'd arrived. As I stood looking around me in the cold air I swayed a little, dizzy with over-tiredness. Snow crunched beneath my feet, and my breath hung weakly in the air. I shivered and pulled my coat tightly around me. Everything was frozen and barren and bleak.

The men went to a door in the smaller of the two buildings and knocked. We were let in by a woman in white wearing a nurse's cap. I couldn't see her clearly because it still wasn't fully light outside but I was relieved, because I knew nurses were kind and compassionate. I was sure she'd give me something to make me feel better.

"Follow me!" she announced, then turned and went back inside.

The two men stood back to let me go first. I had no choice. Clutching my little brown suitcase, I followed her through the open door.

The entrance room was huge. Without losing sight of the woman in white striding ahead of me I tried to take it all in. Coats on hooks lined the walls. Under them were shelves for overshoes; row upon row of overshoes. I'd never seen so many coats and shoes in one place before. How many children could there be here? I hurried by shelves crammed with books. Going past doors to the left and to the right I saw rows of beds with children in them. It was early, and many were still asleep.

The men and I followed the woman in white into a small office. She pushed some papers towards them, which they signed, and then they were dismissed. I didn't like to see them leave. The room seemed colder without them.

I was waiting for the woman to welcome me. I kept thinking, any minute now this lady in white will introduce herself properly and give me a nice warm welcoming smile. Perhaps even a hug. I was really hoping for a loving embrace like my mom would give me. But no. Sitting behind the desk the woman, starched and perfumed, questioned me.

"How old are you?"

As if they didn't already know everything about me.

"I'm eight, Auntie."

The woman in white looked at me coldly. "When you address one of the matrons you will use our proper names. I am Mrs. Norton. Not 'Auntie'. You need to know that right away."

I was confused. She wanted me to call her by her name? Odd Dad didn't know that. I didn't believe her. I always listened to my father, so I resolved I'd call her Auntie, at least until my dad told me otherwise.

"You'll be living here in the annex," she told me. "This is where the younger children reside." She promptly left the room. I wondered if I was supposed to follow her. I could see eyes peering through the glass door in the office, for now the children were getting up and getting ready for school. I was actually looking forward to going to school. It sounded like fun. Some of the children waved at me through the glass. I was too shy to wave back, so looked away, just as the matron returned with an armful of neatly folded clothing.

"These are your new clothes," she said, balancing the stack on a chair.

There was a jacket, some bulky denim jeans, and lots of other things I couldn't make out. The pile was topped by a pair of huge rubber overshoes.

"Every child here has a number assigned to them," she told me. "That way we keep track of what belongs to whom. Your number will be eighty-five. From now on everything you own is to be marked with that number. Every piece of clothing, every sock, shoe, toy, book, pen, hairband; everything."

I couldn't believe what I was hearing.

Hairband?

Pen?!

"You must tell your parents if they buy anything for you they have to put your number on the item. Otherwise you'll have to embroider it yourself."

That frightened me, because I wasn't at all sure what 'embroider' meant. She handed me a laundry pen.

"After you've settled in you'll write your number on everything you've brought with you."

My mind was reeling. I'd just lost my family, and now I'd lost my name too! But no time was given me to process that bombshell, as Mrs. Norton had already moved on to the next one.

"Now, let me acquaint you with the rules," she said. "The first rule is that no Russian is to be spoken here. Under any circumstances."

What! But we're Doukhobors! That's how we Doukhobors pray, and sing, and talk in our community! That's how we speak to each other!

She went on. "You'll be assigned a bed, a dresser, and a locker, all of which are to be kept absolutely clean at all times."

I was light-headed from lack of sleep, and found myself glazing over. Whenever I came to, Matron was still ploughing on with her welcome speech. I hadn't heard anyone talk so much in a long time. Much of the rest of what she said was a blur.

"...will not be tolerated..."

"...very neat and clean..."

"...you will obey your caregivers in everything..."

At last she caught her breath, and stared at me steadily. "If you follow the rules, life here will be pleasant." There was a menacing edge to the way she said 'pleasant'. "However, should you choose to disobey, there will be punishment."

My heart rose to my throat.

Punishment?

"Um, what sort of punishment, exactly?"

"Do as you're told, and you won't have to find out."

My sisters and I were always held to high standards of conduct by our parents and grandparents, but we never doubted that any discipline we received was given because they loved us and cared about our wellbeing. I began to suspect my gentle upbringing had left me ill-prepared to cope with the wider world outside. To my horror, there was yet worse to come.

"Now," she said, "it's time to do something about your hair."

"What do you mean?"

"Take your braids out."

"But I like the way my hair looks."

She clicked her tongue impatiently. "That's beside the point. Here we all try hard to look the same. Your hair must be made to conform with standards that have been set in place."

"What are you going to do?"

She didn't answer, but reached into her desk drawer and pulled out a pair of scissors. My blood ran cold. I couldn't believe what was happening.

"Oh, please Matron, not my hair! Not my beautiful braids! I'm so proud of my hair! I take good care of it. See how silky and shiny it is!"

"Never mind, just do as you're told. We have a nice hairdo here for everyone."

"But I love my hair! I can almost braid it myself! I'll practice every single day. Just let me keep my braids. Please! Please!"

I tried my best to convince her to let me keep my hair. I called her Auntie. I told her I was ugly and that my beautiful hair was the only thing that made me look like a girl.

"Enough of this nonsense! You're far too young to care for such long hair."

I begged her to stop. I promised I'd do my very best to prove I was capable. "Please, please! Just give me a chance!"

There was no changing her mind. I was told to sit down. "We cannot have young children with long hair. It's much too hard to care for."

She threw a towel over my shoulders, then cut off my long, beautiful braids at ear length with two mighty cuts. She hacked off my bangs, and then attacked the back. She cut and cut with no pretence of artistry or even care. I started crying, imagining myself almost bald. The shorn hair stuck to the tears running down my face.

"Stop that at once!"

Not wanting to create trouble for myself, I tried to obey. I'd been there for less than an hour and already I'd learned not to cry out loud. Matron could tell I was still crying though because she could feel my little body shuddering.

"Don't make so much fuss about nothing! This is the way all the girls look here. We want you to feel you belong."

At last the shearing stopped. I was told to go into the bathroom and see what a good job she'd done.

I walked into the girls' washroom feeling sick and exhausted. My stomach was rumbling because I'd thrown up everything I'd eaten in the last three days. And I stank. A couple of girls were standing there, smiling at me. Their eyes were sad though, and I imagined they were remembering their first hours in that place.

When I looked into the mirror I couldn't believe what was staring back at me. I knew it wouldn't be pretty, but this...! My hair, my beautiful hair which used to be my pride and joy, was now reduced to an inept sort of bob. One side was slightly longer than the other. My bangs were crooked. Jagged pieces looking as if chunks had been ripped out stuck up all over the place. It had not been cut, but hacked. It was awful.

I was mortified. I tried hard not to cry again, but how could I not, remembering the little girl in the mirror at home who'd smiled back at me only the day before? Her hair had been beautifully braided by a tender mother, her face had glowed with anticipation. She'd been a happy, well-adjusted girl, loved by those around her. I wondered how she could have so suddenly disappeared, for looking back at me was a frightened child with jagged hair, a green complexion, residual chunks of vomit clinging to her and a face full of tear streaks.

The eyes were dead. There was a sadness around me. I didn't resemble myself anymore. Perhaps I wasn't the same person really, since they'd even taken my name away. My whole being ached to be held in my mother's arms. How would my parents even recognize me when visiting day came? I couldn't believe my misfortune.

"Come along child! You're taking too long."

I ran out of the bathroom, and Matron warned me about running in the buildings. It must have been one of the rules I missed earlier. Is this going to go on for as long as I'm here, I wondered. And how long would that be?

I begged to know when I'd see my parents.

"As I've already explained," she said, rolling her eyes impatiently, "visiting is permitted two Sundays a month. Visits at any other time are strictly forbidden."

"But how soon will I see them?"

"Because last Sunday was a visiting day you'll have to wait two Sundays until the next one."

My heart went numb. It was a Friday. Nine days until I could see my family again. Nine days until I could hug my mother, or laugh with my sisters. I walked behind the matron with my head bent low. Would I ever laugh with my sisters again? A girl I'd not yet spoken to was passing in the corridor, and could clearly see my need for consolation.

"It's okay," the stranger whispered. "Things will be okay. You'll see."

* * *

We returned to the office, where I retrieved my suitcase and dormitory-issue clothing. Mrs. Norton then led me through the doors into the girls' side of the dormitory. I'd never in my short life seen a bedroom so big before. There must have been twelve or fourteen beds in there, some still with sleepy-eyed girls in them.

"Attention, girls!" Mrs. Norton called out. "This is Helen Chernoff. She comes from Grand Forks." A few heads looked up at this new curiosity. Some called out a faint hello to me. Others rolled over and pulled up the covers again. It was much too early in the morning to be getting introduced to anyone.

Mrs. Norton showed me to my bed. "This is where you'll be sleeping," she told me.

There was a small dresser beside the bed, and a locker with the number eighty-five on it. I put my case beside the bed and my pile of clothing on top of the dresser.

"All personal clothing is to be folded neatly in your dresser or properly hung up in your locker. You are expected to keep your dresser and your locker clean at all times. Coats and jackets are to be stored in their proper places in the entrance room. Boots and overshoes go in your number slot."

She was off again. I braced myself for another flood of instructions.

"You will note how the bed is made up," she continued. "The sheets are to be tucked in firmly. The blanket is to be perfectly even on both sides. The corners must be neat. The pillow is to be fluffed up correctly. You are not permitted to keep anything on top of the bed other than one doll or one teddy bear, which will be propped neatly against the pillow when not in use."

My head was spinning. I felt like crying.

"Laundry day is Tuesday. Each week you will put your dirty laundry into the laundry basket. If you miss the laundry you'll have to do it yourself."

One of the girls already up was called over.

"Anna," Mrs. Norton said, "I want you to teach Helen all she needs to know about life here in the annex." Then she turned to me. "Meals are served in the dining hall. Anna will show you where to go."

She turned to leave. Instinctively I said, "Thank you, Auntie."

A collective gasp of horror was heard, and the whole room fell silent. Mrs. Norton continued out of the room. Everyone was looking at me.

"I'm sorry!" I stammered. Clearly I'd done something terribly wrong. I knew we weren't supposed to call the matron 'Auntie', but I'd let it slip without thinking. I never expected the response I got. I tried to remain calm, but inside I was shaking. Oh God, if the staff are mean, please, at least let the girls be nice to me!

I had no idea what to do next. I had new clothes, a number, a new hairdo, and didn't know a single soul. I still felt sick. I'd been grossly mistaken when I'd thought it might be an adventure. I stood still, hoping my head would stop buzzing and that I wouldn't want to throw up anymore.

I heard water running in the sinks, and realized the other girls were getting up. I forced myself to go into the bathroom and start cleaning myself. At the glimpse of myself in the mirror I once again broke down. Lord, help me! I didn't even know who I was anymore, and that after only an hour or so. What would I be like in a week?

After I got back to my bedside some of the girls began to introduce themselves, shyly and one by one. I started looking through the pile of clothing I'd been given. The jackets were blue melton cloth with white piping, and the jeans were heavy, stiff and new. I got out of my dirty clothes and put them on. A bell rang somewhere in the distance.

"That means breakfast is being served," one of the girls told me.

"A bell for mealtimes? You mean like in prison?"

Anna came over. "Follow me," she said, "I'll show you where to go."

As Anna and I left for breakfast, the entrance room swarmed with girls and boys. It turned out that the younger boys slept in a dormitory the same as the girls', but at the other end of the annex, beyond the office. I was far too shy to say hello, or even make eye contact. Some of the girls seemed a little wary of me, anyway. The number eighty-five was already marked on my coat and overshoes. I put them on and followed Anna out of the building.

It was bitterly cold outside, but the fresh air made me realize just how hungry I was. Everything I'd eaten before leaving home was either in a plastic bag or on my dirty clothes back at the annex. We trudged through the snow towards the long, gloomy building I'd seen earlier from the road.

"This is the main dormitory," Irene told me, "where the older children sleep. The boys are on one side and the girls on the other, just like in the annex."

In the centre were the kitchen, and the dining room used by all the children. I couldn't imagine even more children. Where would they fit them all?

I was stunned by the sight that greeted me as I entered the dining room. The place was huge, filled with rows of tables and chairs. There were children everywhere, more than I'd ever seen in one place before. Some looked no older than me, while others were clearly young teenagers. I found it hard to believe that so many children had been removed from their families. There seemed to be about as many boys as girls. The girls sat on one side of the room, and the boys on the other. The older children sat at the far end of the eating area, away from the really young ones. I was always mature for my age, so I found my eyes wandering to the older boys' table. *Hmm, a good selection,* I thought, *if one had a choice.*

Anna showed me my place at one of the younger girls' tables. It was beside a pony wall that separated the children from the matrons.

"You always sit here," she said, "never anywhere else. That way they can tell at a glance who's missing."

There were many introductions, and once again I was anxious. Everyone seemed to know everyone else. I couldn't imagine ever being able to remember each girl's name. Or was that number?

"I wonder what we'll be having for breakfast," I said. The memory of my mother's hot porridge and Grandma's home-made toasted bread made my tummy growl.

"Don't get too excited."

"Why'd you say that?"

"You'll see."

When the food was placed in front of me it wasn't anything I recognized.

"What on earth is this?"

"Some kind of goopy mess they call oatmeal," Anna explained, "and cold dry toast, with milk."

I tried the oatmeal, and it was awful. I gagged, and the vomit rushed up my throat. "Surely we're not expected to eat it!"

"Be quiet," Anna told me. "And if you have to gag, do it so no one can hear."

I thought again of breakfast at home. Mom's oatmeal was hot and good. Borscht, warmed over, was a special treat. I'd never eaten anything this disgusting in my entire life.

"You'd better eat it, or you'll be in big trouble."

I tried hard to swallow the mess on my plate. I was a small girl, and I pictured myself a week or two later just skin and bones, because if that was the kind of food we were expected to eat, I'd die of hunger. Then I worried that if I got really skinny my parents wouldn't recognize me. Imagining my mom's beautiful brown eyes searching for me on visiting day, I somehow managed to get some down and keep it down.

I watched what the other children were doing. Some of them were actually eating the slop. Others deftly scooped the food from their bowls into a sheet of toilet paper, which they then put into a small plastic bag which was quickly slipped into their pockets.

"Psst, Helen! If you can't eat it, always bring toilet paper. Then you can throw it in the bushes on the way to school."

I made a mental note to carry a supply in my pocket at all times.

From where we sat I could see the cooks in the kitchen laughing and smiling. I wondered how they could be so cheerful, given the widespread discontent their food was responsible for.

"They're pretty much all Japanese," I observed.

"There's a Japanese neighbourhood next to the grounds. We walk through it every day on the way to school."

"Don't they know how to cook?"

"It's not their fault. Besides, they're good to us."

"They are?"

"Sure they are! They know what it's like here!"

Meanwhile the matron was wandering between the tables, examining our bowls vigilantly. I became aware that she'd stopped behind me. All conversation at the table ceased.

"You've not finished your food," she observed.

"No, Mrs. Norton." Until I found out why calling her 'Auntie' made the other girls so uneasy, I figured I'd play it safe and do as I was told.

"Why not?"

"I don't feel well. From the trip, and the lack of sleep. And I've been throwing..."

"Do you intend to finish it?"

"I don't think I can."

There was silence. She knew I wasn't lying. The lumps of puke in my hair were evidence enough. I held my breath.

"Children here are expected to finish the food given to them. It is healthful and nutritious." I gingerly pushed the slop around in my bowl with my spoon. It was obvious the matrons didn't eat the same food we did. "However, given the circumstances, you may leave what you cannot finish."

All eyes at the table widened at this apparently unheard-of concession.

"But," Matron snapped, fearful her lenience might be interpreted as compassion, "there will be no more exceptions!"

When breakfast was over, everyone rushed outside. There was lots of yelling and laughter. Snowballs were thrown, and I got hit, really hard, a couple of times. I looked around to see where they'd come from, and a small group of girls from my dorm were staring at me defiantly. I swore to remember their faces so I could get even one day. I wished I'd learned how to fight with the neighbourhood boys in Grand Forks. I wished I could be home. I'd be wishing and wanting until the day I stepped into our home once again. So far it was the longest time in my life that I hadn't seen my mom. I didn't know how I'd be able to live without her. I prayed for the Lord to give me strength, just like Grandma had taught me.

"Helen," Anna said, "I want you to meet my friend Irene."

I turned to see a scrawny girl with a devilish sparkle in her eye. I was shy, but once I met people I could become very chatty, and Irene was warm and friendly. Soon girls were crowding around me.

"Who are you?"

"Where are you from?"

"Who are your parents?"

"Do you have brothers and sisters?"

"Are they here?"

"Tell us what it's like out there."

"How's so and so?"

I was keen to make connections, but as none of the girls was from Grand Forks we didn't have many acquaintances in common.

"Anyway, we can't stand around chatting all day," Anna said. "We have to get ready for school. It's the public one, in town. It's not far, but we have to leave soon."

Never having been in a classroom before, I was excited but also apprehensive. There was so much that was unknown, and it was all happening so quickly. What if the teacher didn't like me? What if the other children picked on me?

One thing at a time Helen... one thing at a time.

When we went back to the annex to collect Anna's school work, Mrs. Norton came over. "You can walk to school with the girls," she said. "When you get there, Anna will take you into class, where you'll be introduced to the teacher."

"Thank you, Aun..." I hastily corrected myself. "I mean, Mrs. Norton."

She turned and left. Again, the same deathly silence filled the room. Again the girls were staring at me, giving looks that could kill.

I turned to Anna. "What's going on?"

She ignored me.

"Please! Tell me what it is."

"Not now."

"Please!"

"I can't."

"Why not?"

"Later."

Desperation gripped me. "No! Tell me now!"

"All right then!" she blurted out. "Some of the girls think you're a spy."

My mouth fell open. "A spy? Why would anyone ever get such a crazy idea as that?"

"Sent here to check up on us."

"What!"

"And then report to the authorities."

I was speechless. "But you don't think that?" I waited. "You don't, do you?" Anna avoided my eyes. "Do you?"

"How do I know why you're here? I've only just met you."

My heart sank. I wanted to curl up and die. After all that had happened in the last twelve hours, I'd thought I couldn't take much more. And now this. Suspected of being a spy by the very girls I'd hoped would accept me! How much worse could it get?

* * *

As we left the annex, I observed how much we all looked alike. We all wore the same blue jackets with white piping, the same baggy jeans, and the same ugly overshoes. My jacket was way too big for me, but I wasn't allowed to wear my coat from home. My overshoes were too big as well. They were the tall ones that came part way up the calf, and walking in them made me feel as if I were wearing snowshoes.

"I've just had an idea," Anna said as we headed out. "Maybe my brother should show you the way to school."

"Your brother? But weren't you going to take me?"

"He's nice. You'll like him."

Anna disappeared for a moment, then returned with a boy. "Helen," she said, "this is my twin brother, Roy." Roy had a warm smile. I assumed he hadn't yet heard I was a possible spy. "He's offered to show you the way to school. Isn't that nice of him?"

The girls nearby all had sly smiles on their faces. I wondered if they knew something I didn't. But I always trusted people. Why would anyone wish me harm?

"Er... I guess so."

We walked through the Japanese village. I marvelled at the small, well-kept houses with lanterns, and the ribbons with strange lettering in the windows, so unlike anything I'd seen in Grand Forks. Distracted by the novelty, it was a while before I realized that Irene and Anna had already scuttled ahead, and I was on my own with Roy.

"We won't be going to school the usual way this morning," Roy told me.

"No? Why not?"

He bent his head close to mine. "Don't make a sound," he whispered. "Just follow me. I'll tell you when it's safe to speak."

"Why?" I whispered back.

"Shhh!"

He started to veer towards the side of the road. Anxiously I followed him.

"It's very dangerous for newcomers to walk to school on the main road. I'll show you the best way, and protect you."

"Protect me?" I asked him. "From what?"

"Shhh!"

"From what?"

"The Old Green Witch Lady who lives just up the road is what. She knows when there's a newcomer to the dorms, and she lies in wait to destroy them."

"She does?"

"You have to be extremely careful not to get caught by her. She's been known to grab the new kids and do unspeakable things to them in the root cellar just behind her house. And because you're new to the dorm you'll have to sneak past her home without making a sound, otherwise she'll come and get you!"

"What if she catches me? What would she do?"

"No one knows," he said. "No one's ever returned to tell."

Not for the first time that day I was gripped by a cold fear. Roy put his finger to his lips. My eight-year-old heart was pounding as if it were about to burst out of my chest.

"What should I do?"

"Luckily, there's another way. We have to sneak past her house so she doesn't hear us, and the only way to do that is to get off the main road and walk through the forest. Then you'll be safe."

I hesitated. The ground on the other side of the ditch was covered with deep snow. Further up the slope, dark trees dotted the ground. Who knew what hungry wild beasts were lurking among them?

"Are you coming?"

"I guess so." *God, please help me!* What had I done to deserve this? *Maybe I should have said all my prayers just as my parents and grandparents taught me. Lord, just help me get through this day,* I begged. *I promise there'll be no more shortcuts in my evening prayers.*

My silent bargaining was interrupted by Roy, who directed me to remove my footwear.

What?!

Didn't he realize it was December in the Kootenays, and everything around us was frozen?

"You'll make less noise that way."

"But won't my feet get cold?"

"Do you want her to hear you?"

Glumly I took my overshoes off and squeezed them into my jacket pockets.

"Not just your overshoes. You have to take off your shoes as well"

"What?!" Oh well, I reasoned, I was already frozen with fear; what was a little more cold? I took my shoes off and hung them round my neck by the laces.

"And your socks."

"She won't hear me in my socks!"

"No, but they'll get wet, and you have to wear them all day. You don't want to be uncomfortable, do you?"

I took off my socks and tucked them into the shoes.

With Roy in the lead and me in my bare feet, we set off. We clambered down into the ditch on the other side of the road, a little way down from the Old Green Witch Lady's house. My insides trembled with fear as I pressed my feet through splinters of ice floating on dark puddles, testing the muddy bottom for sharp twigs and stones. I loved to run barefoot with my sisters behind our parents' house, but that was in soft grass warmed by an August sun. The water in the ditch was so cold it made me gasp. It was almost a relief to clamber into the snow on the other side.

I was terrified the crunch of frozen snow under my feet would give me away. As I stifled a sneeze, aware that any sound might be my death warrant, I worried whether instead I might develop pneumonia and die. How I ever survived the journey is still beyond me. As we walked, Roy kept hunching over ahead of me and making muffled choking noises. I thought he'd caught a chill because he was shaking. It wasn't until later that I realized he was laughing his head off.

Up the slope we went, up, up, across and past the Old Green Witch Lady's house, until we were certain I was well out of her reach. Finally Roy turned to me. "You're in the clear," he said, "so we can go down to the road now. Then you can put on your shoes, if you'd like."

Re-crossing the ditch was easier, as everything below my knees was numb. It was harder though to get my footwear back on when I couldn't feel my feet.

Once back on the main road I found myself among familiar faces. They congratulated me on my close encounter with the Old Green Witch Lady. Roy told me that from then on I could walk freely past her house without fear, just like anyone else. I felt a little happier at the news. But as we approached a wooden bridge over a small river that rushed down from the mountains and fed into the lake, Roy once again took me aside. "Be careful whenever you go by that house on the left," he said. "A weird man lives there. He'll try to grab you and keep you as a slave in his basement."

Here we go again, I thought.

"No, I'm serious. He stands outside his house and shows his pee-pee to the kids walking past. If you make eye contact with him he hypnotizes you, and then you've had it. So don't ever so much as look towards his house, or you'll never see your mom and dad, ever, ever, ever!"

It turned out later that Roy was wrong, at least about the hypnotizing and the basement, but I had no way of knowing it then. So it was with great anxiety regarding the unknown dangers of New Denver that I continued on to face my first day at school.

* * *

We walked over the bridge, past a small convenience store, up a little incline, turned, and there was the school. It looked big, but not as big as the public school in Grand Forks. Never having set foot in a classroom before, I had no idea what to expect, but I was looking forward to it. Because of the way my mother had taught me at home, I had no fear of learning.

Anna presented me to the teacher.

"Good morning. Welcome to New Denver Elementary School. I'm Miss Spencer. What's your name?"

"Good morning, Miss Spencer. I'm Helen Chernoff."

"Ah. You understand English. That's good. What grade were you in when you last went to school, Helen?"

"I've never been to school, Miss Spencer."

"Really? Then we'll have to start you off in Grade One. By the way, how did you learn to speak such good English, Helen?"

My parents had always wanted their children to be completely bilingual, so I was raised to be comfortable speaking either language. If the teacher was delighted I could understand her, the other children from the dorm were amazed. I was one of the very few Doukhobor children to come to New Denver already able to speak fluent English. Most of them were just learning the language.

Miss Spencer was kind, and for the first time that day I felt safe. She introduced me to some of the children from the town, and once again I saw a lot of Japanese faces. She gave me books I didn't have to share with anyone. I thought I'd really delight her, and proceeded to write my name and the number eighty-five on the front. Wow! I did the number without even thinking about it. Guess I'm a pretty fast learner!

"Oh! You can do your letters, as well!" Miss Spencer said.

"Letters? I can write. And read too! "

She was astonished. "In English? How did you ever learn to read and write in English if you've never been to school?"

"My mother taught me. It was fun."

Miss Spencer was mystified. "Then why are you here?"

I decided I liked school, and spent the rest of the day participating enthusiastically. When lessons were over for the morning, we walked back to the dormitory for lunch. I ran ahead and got toilet paper and a plastic bag just in case the food was as bad as at breakfast. When lunch was served I was surprised. It wasn't great, but I managed to keep some down. The rest went into my pocket. I was told the little creatures that lived on our way to school were the best fed in the world.

That afternoon Miss Spencer put on some music for us. "Does anyone here know how to dance?" she asked.

"I do!" I cried, leaping to my feet. "I do!"

I whirled around the room with the teacher to the sound of the music. A few children from the town joined in, but no other children from the dormitory followed. I danced and spun, and became totally lost in the music. I noticed some of the children from the dormitory giving me strange looks, but I couldn't understand why. Possibly they were jealous because I jumped up first. For a few minutes I was in heaven, dancing and humming and smiling, remembering how my sisters and I used to dance at home. All of a sudden the music stopped, and I was brought back to reality. I remembered where I was, and the joy faded.

When school ended I was sorry, because it had been a good day. Well, at least from nine to three. The teacher was friendly, I'd done well in the lessons, and had met some more new faces. My only problem now would be to remember everyone's name. I looked forward to being able to learn with no one yelling at me or bossing me around. After that morning's harsh introduction to the dormitory, my first day at school had given me a sense of freedom. Maybe life in New Denver wouldn't be as bad as I'd feared, after all.

4. SUSPICIONS AND ACCUSATIONS

December, 1955

As the other children and I were walking back to the dormitory after school, I saw in the distance a familiar figure standing on the other side of the bridge. My heart leaped with joy when I realized it was my Grandpa Zebroff.

"Deda!" I cried. "Deda!"

A wave of fear immediately washed over me. Matron had insisted that no visits were permitted outside of the authorized ones every other Sunday. If anyone were to report seeing me with my Grandpa my visiting privileges could be taken away for who knows how long.

I couldn't help myself. I rushed forward and leaped into my Grandpa's arms. I cried and I cried, I was so happy to see him. I hugged and kissed him, relishing the familiar smell of garlic on his breath and the warmth of his arms around me. His beard tickled my face as he kissed me. He squeezed me so tightly I could hardly breathe. I was never so glad to see anyone in my life.

"How ever did you get here, Deda?"

Other children from the dormitory whispered warnings as they walked past. "Be careful," they said. "You'd better not let Matron see you."

Grandpa didn't hear. He stood back and looked at me. "Helen?" he asked in astonishment. "I hardly recognize you! If you hadn't leaped into my arms I'd still be looking for you!"

I didn't know what he meant at first, but then realized the cause of his confusion. I took my hat off and shook out what was left of my hair. He looked at me in stunned silence. Tears came to his eyes. He reached over and gently stroked my hair. "I don't understand. What happened?"

"They want us all to look the same here."

"But how could they do such a thing?"

"It's not just my hair. I've got a number. I'm now known as eighty-five."

The tears froze on Grandpa's face. He became agitated. "Helen! Do you see what they're doing to you?" The children from the dormitory continued to stream past, all looking alike, all wearing the same clothes. "Being numbered is just like in the military," he said. "The government wants to make you all into little soldiers!"

This was Grandpa's worst fear. Fresh tears rolled down his face. He held me close and told me to be strong. My beautiful Grandpa! My heart ached for him. I tried to console him as best I could. "Everything's fine, Deda! They feed us well. The matrons are nice. The other kids aren't mean. You mustn't worry about me! I've made really good friends already. I'm sure I'll be very happy here." My first day in New Denver was when I started to tell lies.

My grandfather wasn't convinced. "How could you possibly be happy in such a place?"

"Of course, I miss my family very much! But I'm going to make the best of the situation. And school's good, too! I did lessons in school today. The teacher's very friendly. Oh Deda, you should have seen me dance with the teacher!"

Grandpa gasped as if he'd been hit in the stomach. "You shouldn't dance, Helen," he said. "Under any circumstances." I'd forgotten in my excitement that I was speaking to Grandpa and not my father, who I knew wouldn't have minded. "We don't do that sort of thing," he added gravely. "And besides, you shouldn't leave yourself open for people to judge you."

He was so disappointed in me it made me want to cry. Instead I told him about my overnight ordeal in the police car. He was so sorry when he heard I'd thrown up all the way. He said he'd followed on the Greyhound, just to make sure I'd arrived in New Denver safely.

"Your auntie drove me to the bus station in Grand Forks right after you left with the police. I travelled all night too. We're all very worried about you."

When a child was brought to New Denver the authorities didn't notify the parents, so my family had no way of knowing I'd arrived. The only way was to come and see for themselves.

At that moment I heard the sound of a car approaching.

"Grandpa, hide!" I whispered urgently.

"Hide?" He was puzzled. "Whatever for?"

"Hurry, Grandpa! Please!" The sound of the car grew closer. I was afraid it might be someone from the dormitory. "Oh, please, Grandpa! I could be in big trouble!"

He could see I was genuinely distressed, so he quickly looked around for a hiding place. Just before the car came into view he scrambled down into the ditch beside the road, and hid there as it went by. With a strange sense of unreality I realized it was the very same ditch I'd climbed into earlier that day on the way to school. When the car had passed, Grandpa emerged from the ditch brushing loose snow and mud from his coat.

"So, they're good to you here, eh?" He said it with a twinkle but I knew I'd been caught out in my first lie. I realized I'd have to practice a lot more before I could ever hope to do it convincingly.

Grandpa reached inside his coat and handed me a packet of cookies. They were graham wafers, coated with sugar and cinnamon. At home we considered them a special treat.

"Oh! Thank you, Deda!"

If I took them back to the dormitory I might have to explain to the matron how I'd got them, so I ripped the packet open and offered them to the children standing round. Grandpa was clearly not expecting the squeals of delight that came from them as each tried to jam whole cookies in all at once.

"The food in the dorm's pretty bad," one of them explained.

"We're always hungry!"

"Any time there's a chance to eat good stuff, we take it!"

I blushed, and avoided Grandpa's gaze. Caught out in my second lie.

In no time the cookies were all gone, and it was time for Grandpa to leave. I didn't want our visit to be over. I wanted him to stay and talk. I wanted to be held and hugged and kissed. I'd never missed my family so much as I did then.

"I have to leave now if I'm to catch the bus for home," he said sadly.

"Then I want to go with you, Deda! I don't like it here. Please take me home!" I was willing to run behind the bus all the way to Grand Forks, if that was what it took.

"My Helen! I only wish I could! But you know it's impossible."

"Then Deda, tell Mama to hide Kathrine and Marie. Don't let the police bring them to this place!"

"Yes, I'll tell your Mama." Coming from my Grandpa, the assurance made me feel better. I felt confident that was all it would take to keep my sisters out of New Denver. "But you must pay attention to what your caregivers tell you. And be obedient at all times."

I kissed him goodbye. "I'll do my best, Deda. Tell the family I'm all right. I don't want them to worry about me."

We wished each other goodbye amid sobs and tears.

"Goodbye, Deda! I'll see you a week from Sunday!"

A few more hugs and kisses from him, and he was gone.

From then on my grandfather came only on visiting days. This unauthorized visit was the only time in all my years in New Denver that I saw anyone from my family without matrons, guards and police present.

"Come on!" the girls called out. "They always count to see no one's missing."

I hurried to catch up to the rest of the children. I'd have to get back to the dormitory before someone noticed, or worse, before someone reported I'd had a visit.

The afternoon was bitterly cold. I was very careful not to look in the direction of the house where the weird man lived. I finished the walk back to the dormitory, straight past the Old Green Witch Lady's house, with no fear whatsoever, but with my heart and soul aching for home and for my family. My hands were numb. My feet still hurt from walking barefoot in the snow earlier in the day. Waves of dizziness had been sweeping over me from time to time throughout the day, due to the lack of sleep the night before. And now I wanted to cry because my grandpa had gone home.

On arriving back at the sanatorium a child ran up to me. "Are you Helen Chernoff?"

"Yes."

"Matron says she wants to see you in her office right away."

My hear sank. Someone must have reported my visit with Grandpa. My first day, and already I was in trouble.

My stomach churned with fear as I knocked on the door of Mrs. Norton's office. She barked, and I stepped inside.

"Stand there, Helen." While she worked with papers at her desk I wondered what my fate would be. At last she looked up. "I told you this morning we like to do things properly here. Maybe you're not entirely clear about what that means."

My head swam and my knees went weak. I feared I'd never see my family again.

I needn't have worried. Nobody had told her about my meeting with Grandpa. She just wanted to give me more rules about the conduct expected of us in the dormitory. The rules were long-winded, but were mostly just plain common sense. Apparently we wouldn't be allowed to steal or swear or cheat or fight. I wondered where she thought we were raised. Our parents had taught us right from wrong. I didn't need this woman telling me stuff I already knew.

When I came out some of the other children came over to me.

"How are you doing?"

"I'm okay."

"Are your feet still cold?"

"Don't be mean!" said Anna. "It's her first day. Come on! We'll show you round the place."

I'd only seen the dormitory buildings that morning before it was fully light, and when I'd hurried in for lunch. Now I had time to take it all in, I saw that the main building, which housed the older children and the dining room, actually had very attractive verandahs along the front. The back of the building had a magnificent view of Slocan Lake, only a few yards away, and of the mountains beyond.

The girls were curious about me. Some were openly hostile. "Are you a spy?" one of them asked, getting straight to the point.

"Of course not!"

"Then why were you reporting on us to Matron just now?"

"I wasn't reporting anything. She was just telling me some more stupid rules."

"But how come you get to have a visit with your grandpa, then? You must be a spy, to get special privileges like that"

"I'm not a spy!"

"Then why would they send you here when you can already speak English?"

"I'm here for the same reason you are - my family are Freedomites."

"We're here because our parents refused to send us to school."

"So am I."

"Then how come you can speak English, if you never went to school?"

"I learned it at home. We all speak Russian and English at home. Except for my Baba."

"Why?"

"It was just something we did."

* * *

Across from the main dormitory was the annex, the smaller building where I'd be sleeping. A laundry stood nearby; I could see steam escaping through cracks in the walls and out of a vent in the roof. Between the main dormitory and the laundry there was a gymnasium. I looked through the glass panels in the doors. Nets hung from the wall above a hardwood floor that was incredibly shiny.

"Do we ever get to use this?"

"Sure. We take extra gym all the time. They don't like us doing nothing."

It sounded like a good idea to me. I really liked sports.

Underneath the snow, I was told, was the ball diamond. I recalled for a brief moment playing a kind of soccer-and-baseball with my mom and sisters at our home in Grand Forks. My heart surged, and suddenly I wanted to cry.

My questioners were determined not to let me off the hook so easily.

"But is it true you can read and write English, too?"

"Mom taught us all to read and write in English. It was part of our lessons."

"What lessons?"

"My Mom taught us lessons at home."

"But Doukhobors don't believe in education."

"My parents do! My parents believe in expanding our minds."

"They mustn't be Freedomites, then."

"But we are!"

We walked around to the front. As we approached the entrance to the grounds I noticed a tiny building with someone inside it.

"What's that?"

"It's the guard shack."

I recalled the figure in the darkness as I'd arrived that morning.

"There's a man in there all the time. He keeps an eye on us as we come and go."

I didn't understand. "But the grounds are wide open. We could come from any direction."

"Well... I think they're there to make sure we don't do anything bad."

"Like what?"

Nobody really seemed to know.

"Maybe the guards are there for our protection," someone put in.

Now I was concerned. "Why would we need protection? Who from?" I was glad my parents didn't know about it, or they'd really be worried.

"They say you danced at school with the teacher. Is that true?"

"Sure I did!" I could see no harm in what I'd done. After all, we used to dance at home whenever we wanted.

"But Doukhobors don't dance."

"But we do!"

"No we don't! It's dancing with the devil. You'll go to hell!"

"But we do! We're all the same people. Our parents just do things differently."

I was thinking it had to be a bad dream and I was going to wake up to feel my mom's kisses on my face. I decided the only way to find out was to pinch myself. I did, and let out a yelp.

"What happened?"

"I stepped on a rock." *I guess this has to be for real then*, I thought.

"But why did you call the matron 'Auntie'?"

"I didn't want to, but my dad told me I had to."

"Why would he do that?"

"Unless you're a spy, of course."

"I'm not a spy!" I wanted to scream. "I was taught to call all older people 'Auntie' and 'Uncle'. It's a form of respect."

"Respect?" the kids chorused. "Respect? These bitches don't deserve any respect!"

I was shocked. I couldn't believe what I was hearing.

"They beat us, wash our mouths out with soap, punish us in every way possible. Fuck the respect!"

My jaw dropped. I didn't know Doukhobors spoke like that. I'd certainly never heard language like that in my family. The worst I'd heard was the odd 'damn', when Auntie Vatkin would swear at Uncle Mike when he got drunk. I had no intention of speaking like that, and I certainly wasn't going to curse the matrons the way other girls did.

Suddenly the dinner bell rang, and we all scrambled towards the dining room. My stomach was growling from hunger, but at least I didn't feel like throwing up anymore. I was filled with a desperate hope that the meal would be good. It wasn't, and I wasn't really surprised. Everything except the bread was awful. Despite my enthusiasm I'd come prepared for the worst. I stuffed the food into my pocket and ate more bread, with lots of butter on it. I figured if the food never improved I could eat bread and butter every day as long as I was there. I hoped it wouldn't be for very long.

We had playtime after supper. The first thing we did was to get rid of the food in our pockets. I'm sure the little animals appreciated it, because there wasn't a lot of food for them with snow on the ground. I helped some of the other children make a snowman. Coming in when playtime was over I remembered to hang up my coat and put my overshoes in the space marked '85', as I'd been told to do.

I then learned the rules about getting ready for bed. We had to turn down the bedcovers perfectly, get our pyjamas on, then brush our teeth and our hair. Matron gave us cod liver oil on a teaspoon, and I gagged. It was even worse than the food we'd just tried to eat at dinner.

We took turns showering a couple of times a week. That first day was one of my days. Although I was eager to get cleaned up, I was uncomfortable about the idea of standing in front of the other girls totally naked. I whined a little to Matron, who just told me to get undressed and into the shower. When I hesitated she started to remove my clothes, and I finished.

The girls in the bathroom looked at my naked body.

"How come you're so skinny?"

One of them pointed at me. "She's got no boobs," she laughed. "She looks like a boy!"

What a bunch of idiots, I thought. *What do they expect of an eight-year-old?*

I stepped into the shower. I couldn't believe three of us were expected to try and get ourselves clean in such a small space.

"It only runs for five minutes, and then it's turned off," one of the girls told me helpfully.

"What if you still have soap in your hair, or in your eyes?"

She shrugged. "Too bad."

"What if you can't get under the shower because someone else is in the way?"

"Then you've got to learn to use your elbows!"

I wasn't sure how to wash my hair, because my mom had always washed it for me. So even though I looked ugly with my new short hairstyle, I had to admit five minutes wouldn't have been enough time for me to wash it on my own. After the shower I crawled into bed. We had a few moments to read. *How stupid*, I thought irritably. *Most of these girls don't even know how to read.*

I lay awake after lights out and thought about what had happened since I'd left home just over twenty-four hours earlier. My whole life had changed in that time, and a new routine was already firmly in place. I hoped I could remember everything I had to do, because I didn't want to get into trouble. The main rule to remember was that Matron was always right, and never to argue with her.

I thought about my home and my family. Deda would still be travelling home on the bus. I wondered if Baba was lonely without him? What did everyone eat for supper? I missed Mom's cooking already. Kathrine and Marie would be in bed by now. Did Mom read them a bedtime story? Did they get hugs and kisses? Were they giggling together? Did they get cookies for a snack before bed? I was hungry, but we weren't allowed to eat except at mealtimes. I didn't know how I'd survive, as I liked to eat all the time.

I could hear whispering. Matron came in and told the girls to be quiet. Then there was a commotion from the boys' side, and Matron went running over there. Harsh words ensued, followed by silence.

There were so many things I'd have to learn to do just to survive. Learn to lie. I knew that would be hard for me to do. I'd been raised to tell the truth at all times, but from then on I figured I'd say what I thought others wanted to hear. I'd have to learn to be strong, so no more crying. I'd have to get used to eating that garbage they called food or I'd starve to death in no time. I'd have to figure out a way to speak Russian without getting into trouble. And if I got caught doing wrong I'd better learn real quick how to talk my way out of punishment.

I wished I could find a book that could unteach all the values I'd been taught. I'd watch those around me, and learn from them what I couldn't teach myself. I'd tell my family all was well even when it wasn't. Especially when it wasn't. There was no need to worry them. They couldn't do anything about it anyway. The only thing I'd allow myself to tell them was that I wanted to go home.

Home. Home is supposed to be a safe place, filled with love. Welcome to your new home, Helen.

I was exhausted, and at last the events of the day receded, and sleep took over. Sometime later I woke, whimpering and weeping. Someone yelled at me to shut the hell up. In my dreamlike state I reminded myself again never to cry in front of anyone. I didn't want to be known as a crybaby. I sure didn't want the other children to think I was weak, or they'd pick on me. I'd only allow myself to cry when I was saying goodbye to my family. Hungry and alone, I fell asleep again, longing for home, and yesterday.

5. LIVING FOR VISITING DAY

December, 1955

When I woke the next morning it was still dark. Matron bustled in and turned on the lights. "Up, up up, everyone!" She looked at me. "Will someone show Helen how to make the bed?"

Irene volunteered. "Watch what I'm doing, and copy me," she said.

We quickly brushed our teeth and hair, and washed our faces. Then the lesson began.

"Make sure the sheet's really tight," Irene said, "and then tuck the corners in. Matron wants a perfect triangle - just like in the army."

I pulled the corners so tightly I thought I was going to rip the sheets.

"Not like that. Tighter!"

This was all new to me. I'd never made a bed in my life.

"Now stretch out the blanket, and tuck it in. Tighter!"

I was struggling. The bedding was bigger and heavier than me.

"Now the bedspread. Make sure it's really, really tight!"

I persevered, determined to get it right.

"Fold your pyjamas. Plump up the pillow."

Done!

"Make sure there's nothing on the bed, and the dresser is clear of junk."

Done!

I was quite proud of myself when I was finished. The first bed I'd ever made, and it was textbook perfect!

Suddenly I became aware that the room had fallen silent. I turned to see Mrs. Norton standing in the doorway. All the girls were standing to attention beside their beds. Irene motioned me to do the same.

Mrs. Norton was so starched I wondered how she could even move. Her nurse's dress was white and crisp, her shoes were polished way beyond what was necessary to cause temporary blindness, and she had a perm in which every curl kept religiously to its assigned place. She wore a Ferrari-red lipstick that made her look very glamorous. I hoped one day I'd be able to have a perm and red lipstick; then thought I'd probably go to hell for even thinking like that, because Doukhobors didn't wear makeup or go to the beauty parlour to get their hair done. Well, except Auntie Vatkin. My mom just brushed her hair back and put it in a ponytail or a braid. Mrs. Norton's fingernails were bright red as well, and looked simply stunning. I longed to do that, but I could hear Grandma Zebroff's shocked response already. 'We don't do that.'

She came around slowly, inspecting each girl's newly-made bed. She stopped by one of them. The girl standing beside it suddenly turned pale. Mrs. Norton stretched out her arm and dropped a coin on the bed. It bounced on the taut bedcovers as if it were a rubber ball. When it came to rest she picked it up and moved on without a word. The girl swallowed heavily, then breathed again.

At the next bed Matron stopped by, the coin didn't bounce. She stripped the bed and told the girl to remake it. We all stood tense until the unfortunate girl had re-tightened her bedcovers and the coin bounced high enough to satisfy Matron.

Mrs. Norton continued around the room. My heart was in my throat as she approached my bed. She dropped the coin. It bounced, a little. I prayed that maybe because I was new she'd be lenient with me. She retrieved the coin - a dime - from my bedspread, and then, with a dramatic wave of her arm, ripped the covers from my bed. My beautiful newly-made bed! I could swear she had a smirk on her face.

Flustered, I fumbled to remake the bed. When I'd finished and was standing, trembling, to attention she dropped the coin again. My heart sank as she ripped my bed apart, again. Again, I remade the bed. Again, she dropped the coin. I couldn't bear to look. Finally the bitch left me alone, and went on to torment the next girl.

I couldn't believe the words I'd learnt to use in the past twenty-four hours. I kind of liked to swear. It was, of course, forbidden, but what they didn't know certainly couldn't hurt me. And, as far as I knew, Matron couldn't read my mind, so I continued to cuss in my mind.

Bitch! Bitch! Bitch!

* * *

The rest of that first week I spent every possible moment trying to convince the other children I wasn't a spy. My dad's insistence that I call all the caregivers 'Auntie' hadn't made the task any easier.

Irene was the first to listen to me. We talked and we talked, and finally, when my mouth was dry from talking, she said she believed me. Relief poured over me. She then tried to convince the others I wasn't a spy but a true daughter of staunch Freedomite Doukhobors, just like the rest of them. It took a few more days, though. Until Irene came forward they circled me like vultures. Finally, due to her persistence, most of them accepted I was just like them except that I could read, write and speak English. Life became easier then. I started to make my first friends in the dormitory, and before long I was also making friends at school.

There was a pecking order among the children though, and that was a hard role to learn. The bigger and badder and meaner you could be, the easier it was to survive. I was neither mean nor tough, and I certainly wasn't bad. I did however have a big mouth and a firm grasp of the English language, and learned very quickly how to use that big mouth to my advantage.

Although she was so glamorous, Mrs. Norton was scary to look at. I soon learned I was right to be afraid of her. Strapping on the wrist was the usual punishment in the dormitory, and those who'd received it told me it was extremely painful. So I resolved to be on my very best behaviour, at least until such time as I could talk or lie my way out of a situation.

Each morning I dutifully made up my bed, dusted my dresser and made sure there wasn't a single item out of place. One day during my first week I went to the annex after lunch to get something from my locker. When Mrs. Norton saw me she stormed over.

"Were you raised in a pigsty?" she demanded. Before I could answer she took me by the ear and dragged me over to my bed. "Is this the way you live at home?"

I looked at my bed. There was a scattering of other girls' sweaters and combs and random personal belongings on it.

"Here we put our things away like civilized people."

"But these aren't mine," I protested.

"This is your bed?"

"Yes, Mrs. Norton."

"You were told to keep it tidy?"

"Yes, Mrs. Norton."

"Then do so."

When she was gone I looked at the numbers marked inside the clothing, as she could easily have done had she chosen to. The items belonged to Hazel Tarasoff and Alice Postnikoff, who had the beds either side of me. I folded their clothing and placed it neatly in their dressers with the other articles and left. I had no idea why their things should have been on my bed. At first I assumed it was a mistake.

But then it happened again.

"Did your mother never teach you anything?" matron raged.

"But..."

"This is your final warning. If it happens again you'll be receiving the strap!"

I didn't know why Hazel and Alice wanted to see me in trouble, but I knew I didn't want to get the strap. I'd heard girls talk about it in hushed tones. It wasn't entirely clear from what they'd said whether it could actually be fatal or not, but I sure didn't want to be the one to find out. The next morning I waited in the bathroom until after Hazel and Alice had gone for breakfast. When I came out the same mess as before was scattered all over my bed. I took their stuff and threw it back on their beds, where it belonged. I did a messy job. Then I tightened my blanket and off I went.

Boy, did the girls ever get it, because they'd been here longer than me and should have known the rules better.

When they got outside they came looking for me, but before they could say anything I exploded.

"How dare you put your things on my bed?!" I yelled.

They stopped, open-mouthed. Other girls nearby looked up at the commotion.

"We were just having..."

"Don't interrupt!" My teeth were clenched. I could feel the skin tighten around my cheekbones. "I don't know why you think you have permission to treat a new girl like that," I barked, "but you don't!"

They looked confused. Permission?

"And if this ever happens again, I'll take whatever's on my bed and throw it in the garbage! Is that understood?"

They breathed uncomfortably. I guess I looked pretty fierce. I may even have sounded a little like matron.

"Is that understood?"

They wilted.

"Um... sorry."

I learned that day that a few well-chosen words can sometimes be way stronger than actions. I could never recall answering back to my parents, and wouldn't dream of mouthing off the matrons. But I sure did use those to establish my place with the rest of the children. I really had to watch carefully though, because even if I threatened the girls it was entirely up to me to see they didn't put their junk on my bed. If they did I would be the one in trouble, and they'd merely laugh at me when I got punished. But for the moment my bluff was working. From that day not even a stray bobby pin found its way onto my bed.

* * *

Days went by slowly, and the twin yearnings to go home and to eat something good were constantly on my mind. Breakfast wasn't too bad when we had boiled eggs and toast, but when they made runny porridge with lumps that looked like snot my stomach felt like turning inside out. I'm not sure how I managed to get it down and then keep it down, but it was that or go hungry. The rest was thrown into the ditch on the way to school.

Dinner was usually just as bad, and my mouth watered every time I thought of food from home. Because Doukhobors don't eat meat, all our meals were vegetarian. The Japanese cooks didn't know what we were used to eating, and even if they did they couldn't be blamed for not knowing how to prepare it. In that first week I wrote to my family and begged my mom to make some of her delicious borscht and pyrahi for me, and to bring them on visiting day.

I missed my mom terribly. My heart ached for her kisses, I wanted to feel her lips brush my cheek, I wanted her to stroke my hair and give me hugs. I missed my sisters Kathrine and Marie, too. We'd always shared great secrets that we kept from everyone. There was no one in New Denver I could share anything with. I missed the joy we had together. It didn't take much for the three of us to be howling with laughter from nothing at all. I missed sharing bedtime stories, and giggling until we fell asleep together in our big old cozy bed.

Silent tears ran down my cheeks as I lay in the dark and remembered. I wondered if they missed me the way I missed them. But I'd promised myself I wouldn't cry. It was a sign of weakness, and I didn't need to be beaten up just because of my tears. As the newest person I figured I'd have to bear the brunt of the jokes and teasing for a while, but I told myself to be strong. Sooner or later someone new would arrive, and then I'd be left in peace.

I felt so alone. I'd met some of the girls, and a couple of the boys, but I didn't really know them yet. Others walked around me, pointed at me, and whispered quietly. A few still believed I was a spy, and told me I'd burn in hell for my wrongdoing. They were harsher than the matrons, watching me like a hawk, waiting for me to make a mistake. To them I was still an outsider.

Sometimes the girls I was with would tell the boys teasing me to go to hell, and the boys would back off. I wished I could be brave like them but I was afraid. I'd never known real fear in my entire eight years, but now I ran on fear from the moment I opened my eyes in the morning until sleep overtook me at night. Even then the fear never left me. There was no talking allowed after lights out, but some of the girls did anyway. One evening after we were all in bed somebody said something funny and the whole girls' side of the annex erupted into laughter. The matron stormed in and demanded to know who started it. Of course we all pretended to be sleeping. But then more laughter escaped from under the covers. The matron pulled a couple of girls from their beds and made them stand in the shower stall all night long. They were exhausted, but every time they lay down to sleep, the matron would go in and wake them up again. It was lonely and sad for these children. There was nothing they could do but resign themselves to their punishment.

I was warned that as well as the matrons, the guards were pretty mean too.

"Except for Tadi, of course," someone piped up.

"Who?"

"Who?! You mean you haven't yet met Tadi?"

It was explained to me that Tadi was the affectionate nickname for Tad Mori, a Japanese man from the village who worked at the sanatorium as a guard.

"If you ever need a friend you can count on Tadi."

My new friends led me over to the shack to meet him one day after school. For the first time since I'd arrived, an adult from the dormitory smiled warmly at me and extended his hand in a gesture of goodwill. His eyes were friendly, and I liked him from the start.

I was still confused by the idea of guards watching us though. I thought you only had guards at a prison. Maybe the New Denver sanatorium was meant to be a kind of prison for us. But that still didn't explain why we were there. I didn't believe you could be sent to jail just for not attending school. Sometimes I thought maybe it was punishment for being mean to my little sisters. I remembered reading murder mysteries to them, and changing my voice according to the character, to scare the hell out of them. But I couldn't recall doing something so bad my parents would have to send me away. It was strange. I felt like a criminal, but I also knew I hadn't done anything really wrong.

My parents hadn't told me how long I'd be away. I hoped it wouldn't be for very long. I hoped they'd miss me a whole bunch, and come and get me.

The days rolled on, one into the other, and visiting day was fast approaching. By Saturday I could feel the excitement. We were all looking forward to the next day, drooling about the food our parents were going to bring. A couple of the children would be sitting on their beds during the visit. My heart ached for them, not being able to see their parents when everyone else was visiting and eating. I reminded myself not to complain to my parents when they came; they'd only worry about me. *Put on your sunny face*, I told myself. God would forgive me for lying if I did it to protect them from the truth.

That Saturday evening the large room at the entrance to the annex used as an indoor playroom became a movie theatre. Benches were set up in rows, with boys on one side and girls on the other. The older children from the main dormitory were there too.

I felt kind of worldly as I casually mentioned I'd been to a movie before. "My grandpa once took me to the theatre in Grand Forks to see a Russian movie," I told them. "It had English subtitles." I'd been very proud of myself because I could read the subtitles and listen at the same time.

Irene said they often got to see a movie on Saturday nights. "And we're allowed to choose the ones we want to see," she added.

"Really! You mean, anything?"

"But they're usually cowboys and Indians. The boys outvote us."

We each had to pay five cents to see the movie. I was willing to break the dollar my auntie had given me before I left home. That meant I'd still have ninety-five cents left over. Some of the children didn't have the five cents. I didn't feel like sharing. The children who didn't have money had to stay in their dormitories until the movie was over. The movie was a western. The boys were screaming and yelling, cheering on the good guys. I didn't like all the shooting and killing, but it was exciting to be part of the group.

Boy, my grandparents wouldn't have liked it if they'd known what I was watching!

* * *

At last, Sunday arrived. The feeling of joy was tangible. We were all careful to be on our best behaviour, knowing the slightest mistake might yet cost us a visit. Beds were made to perfection. We ate breakfast, and then the wait began.

"I guess they'll be here soon," I said.

"Our parents? They don't get here till this afternoon."

"What! You mean we don't get the whole day with them?"

"The whole day?" Irene laughed. "No, visiting's just from one till two."

"What!"

I could hardly believe my ears.

One little hour? Impossible!

That wasn't nearly enough time! How would I ever fit in everything I want to tell my parents, and catch up on what was happening at home, in such a short time? The rest of the morning dragged. I longed to see my family. It had only been ten days since I'd left home, but it felt as if I hadn't seen them in years.

After lunch we were finally allowed to line up outside in front of the annex. The older girls had set up a table with bread, salt and water on it, according to Doukhobor custom. Beyond the entrance the road sloped gently uphill past the low houses of the Japanese village. Behind us Slocan Lake wound its way around the town. We stood in the snow facing the main road, boys to one side and girls to the other, and watched the road for our parents' arrival.

From where we stood I could almost see the Cape. This was the elevated stretch of highway that ran alongside the lake, and led to home. It was the route we'd taken when I was first brought to New Denver. It was narrow there, and drivers had to pull over to let other cars pass. That made it dangerous enough in the summer, but with the ice and snow in winter it was treacherous. I prayed my family had made it through safely. I prayed they wouldn't all die in a mass of twisted wreckage just for coming to visit me.

Suddenly I became aware of a faint sound of singing coming from a long way off. Even before I could be sure I wasn't imagining it I recognized it as a Doukhobor song I'd known since childhood; a familiar song of hope and trust in the Lord. My heart swelled with joy. I found myself singing along. All the other children spontaneously started to sing too. I craned my neck to see where the singing was coming from.

Then our parents appeared, walking together towards us down the little rise from town. My eyes searched desperately for my mom. I couldn't see her anywhere. I was trying to sing and search at the same time. What if none of my family could make it because of the snow? God, please let me see my mom!

Our families stopped before the guardhouse, men on one side and women on the other. The stirring voices of men, women and children continued to fill the air. Everyone was crying. I wasn't. I was happy because I was about to see my family.

And then, like a miracle, I saw my mother's beautiful face! And there was my dad! There, my auntie and grandparents! Where were my sisters? Hidden, I guessed, by those in front. I couldn't wait for the song to end so I could be with them. Damn! Now we were starting another song! Did our parents not realize how desperate we were for them?

At last the hymns and prayers came to an end, and we ran to join our families. My mom hadn't seen me, and was caught off guard as I flung myself at her. I was in heaven as both my parents enfolded me in their loving arms. My grandparents and auntie covered my face with their kisses. My sisters squeezed inside my parents' embrace to hug what bits of me they could. The affection of my family overwhelmed me. I couldn't help myself, and the tears poured down my cheeks.

I stood back to look at my parents. They stared in astonishment.

"Helen!"

"You look so different!"

"We couldn't tell it was you!"

"Deda told us they'd cut your hair, but..."

My mom started to cry. She turned to my dad.

"What have they done?"

I answered their flurry of questions, mostly with half-truths. "Everything's okay," I told them. "I'm settling in quite well." I didn't want to talk. I didn't want to tell them the matrons were cruel. I didn't want to tell them the other children had thought I was a spy. I didn't want to tell them I was starving because I couldn't bear to eat the food we were served. There was no point telling them anything, except a few good things, like the boiled eggs, and school. In return I had only one question for them: "What did you bring to eat?"

"Can we not go inside, first?" Auntie Vatkin asked.

Other families had moved away, and were already spreading out blankets on the snowy ground.

"I don't think so."

"We're expected to sit in the snow?"

"I'm sure we can manage," Grandpa said gently.

Grumbling at the injustice, Auntie Vatkin found an empty space, and prepared it as if for a summer picnic from the basket my father was carrying. We were all dressed warmly, but even so we had to wrap ourselves in blankets against the bitter wind off the lake. I sat snuggled up to my mother, a blanket wrapped around us both.

Mom opened a thermos and handed it to me. My mouth watered at the unmistakable aroma. Borscht, hot and delicious! For a moment the cold didn't bother me. I gulped down as much as I could, trying not to burn my mouth. My family didn't eat, only I did. Then Mom handed me a container with warm pyrahi, covered in melted butter. Oh, I could hardly believe my good fortune! I remembered there was just one hour and then the visit was over. My family stared at me as I wolfed down the food. Then for dessert my mother produced some of her fresh doughnuts, followed by fruit, and then cake. I was in heaven. I ate without chewing. When I finished I was so full I could hardly sit. I loosened my belt.

There were about a dozen policemen around the guard shack during visiting hour. I had no idea why they were there. Maybe they were going to arrest someone. I sure hoped it wouldn't be me, because, except for the things I'd done to survive in the past week or so, I really hadn't done anything wrong.

"When am I going to go home?" I asked.

"We have to wait this out," my father replied, "see what happens."

"But I don't like it here!"

My father said nothing.

"I could go to school in Grand Forks, and come home for lunch every day. I promise I'll study hard. I'll make you so proud of me! Please, just let me come home!"

My father remained tight-lipped. "It's not possible to do that right now."

I'd always known my parents and my family loved me. Deep down in my heart though, I began to suspect maybe they didn't love me anymore. Why else would they send me away and leave me to fend for myself? It was a horrible suspicion for a young child to have. I felt a bitterness towards my parents I'd never felt before. How could they not love me? I'd been such a good girl, except during the past week or so. Maybe if I told the truth about life in the dormitory they'd take me home with them. But I couldn't, because then they'd worry about me, and I'd much rather believe my parents didn't care about me than make them worry.

Families around us started getting up and folding their blankets.

"No! Not yet!" I cried. The hour had gone by so quickly I couldn't believe it.

My mother wrapped up the remains of the cake and put it in my coat pocket. "Please, Helen, take care of yourself!" she said.

There was a lot of crying going on. I was crying too, because I wanted my parents to take me home with them and they wouldn't. Again I asked why not, but this time there was no reply. Just the same tight jaws, the same stiff lips. I held onto my mom. If I didn't let go maybe she'd just drag me along with her and no one would even notice. Dad told me again and again to behave, and to pay close attention to the matrons so I wouldn't get into trouble

The families formed up as before, with the men to the left and the women to the right. The children formed up facing them. The hymns started again, and we all joined in. They started moving away. Goodbye for two more weeks. And then, if I behaved and didn't get my visiting privileges taken away, I'd see my family again, for one hour. I was bawling as I watched my parents leave. The mournful sound of Russian prayer became weaker as our families moved farther and farther away. Some parents turned and waved goodbye, others didn't. My mom did. One by one the children fell silent. At last we were left alone with just the quiet, biting cold of the wind off the lake. It was early afternoon and visiting day was already over.

"Move quickly, children!"

Matron needed us to stand at the foot of our beds immediately, so she could check whether anyone was missing.

It all felt like a dream, or rather a nightmare. One miserable little hour, and a lot of that spent singing. One hour, twice a month. I couldn't live like that! I was sure my parents would forget about me. I'd be remembered as their lost child, if I was remembered at all. After the head count we sat around and exchanged stories. Some of us were still crying, but softly so the matron couldn't hear us. We were all aware that life was going on as before in the outside world, and that we were no longer a part of it.

6. FINDING MY FEET
December 1955

After the first visit a girl approached me. Her name was Sophie, and she resided in the big girls' dormitory. Those girls were thirteen and older. A couple were almost fifteen, and ready to go home as soon as their birthdays came around. Fifteen was the magic number for us, because it was legal to quit school at that age. Sophie was beautiful and looked very grown up. She reminded me of a movie star. Or at least what I believed a movie star should look like. She said that because I was so young and inexperienced, my family had asked her to look out for me. If there was any sort of trouble, or if anyone picked on me, I was to let her know.

I was a little peeved, because after only a week in the dorms I figured I was doing a pretty good job of looking after myself. I could swear really well by now, and that scared some of the 'fraidy cat kids. I didn't swear when my parents were there. Or at school. Well, I did at school, but not when the teacher could hear me. On the other hand, I had to admit it felt special having someone so much older and wiser taking an interest in me. I don't know how it was my parents picked Sophie. If I needed protection they should have asked Doris or Lisa, because they were the two toughest girls in the dorms. Doris and Lisa didn't take flak from anyone. In the short time I'd been there those two had already received by far the most punishments.

Fortunately for me, Sophie had a very sensitive nature. When I needed help I'd go to her and she was always very kind to me. She brushed my hair, and often brushed my fears away too. In a way she became my mother away from home. I think my auntie used to slip her a dollar or two in appreciation of what she was doing.

* * *

All of the children in the sanatorium spoke Russian, and many had very limited or no ability in English. Some refused to speak except in Russian, and so had their mouths washed out with soap. After that they tried to learn English, but often had no idea how to say what they needed. My heart ached for them. I could only imagine how difficult it must have been to try and understand what the teachers at school were telling them. How much more terrifying to have a hostile matron towering over them and yelling in a foreign language, unable to understand a word being said. In those situations I found myself instinctively taking on the role of unofficial translator, especially for the younger ones and for recent arrivals.

One time a girl wanted her bangs cut. She didn't know how to say it in English, so she used the Russian word. "Please, Matron," she said, "could you cut my choop?"

The matron thought she was crazy; but I translated, the bangs were cut, and the girl was given heck for using Russian.

Well, a whole new adventure began. I did a lot of translating in school, at the dorm, and even when playing with some of the children from the town. Mainly the girls just wanted one or two words to get their point across to the matron, but sometimes I was needed to translate whole sentences. Once I had their trust I was in demand to translate all kinds of things. Someone wanted help writing a letter. Another needed a new pair of shoes because the old ones didn't fit.

I enjoyed the prestige this gave me, remembering the struggle I'd had to convince everyone I wasn't a spy. And I can't deny feeling a twinge of disappointment when other children's English gradually improved and my services were no longer needed so much. But by then my need for acceptance had been replaced by a great sense of belonging. In my heart I knew that this group of children was going to be my family for as long as I was in the dorm. And at last I was one of them.

One day, following a particularly heavy snowfall, we all rushed back after school.

"Come on," my girl friends called out excitedly.

"What's happening?"

"You'll see. And keep your boots on!"

We all gathered behind the main dormitory in the free time before dinner. It got dark early in late December, and the overhead floodlights that lit up the grounds at night were already on. We spread out on a level patch of ground beside the verandah on the boys' side, close to the lake. There must have been close to a hundred of us. Then we started trampling the snow, stomping back and forth.

"What are we doing?" I asked the girl beside me.

"Have you ever skated before?"

"No."

"It's great fun. You'll love it!"

"We're making a rink?"

"Just keep stomping!"

The wind was chilly and my legs were sore, but I didn't stop because I was eager to learn how to skate. We did this for a couple more days, after school. When the snow was well trampled, then came the fun part. Someone got a garden hose, turned the water on full blast, and flooded the area with water. The water froze almost as soon as it hit the snow. When it was good and solid we hosed it down again, and then again. Sometimes whoever was holding the hose turned and sprayed those of us who were watching. The water turned to ice on our faces, but we didn't mind because we knew in a few days we'd be skating.

At last the ice was ready, and we had a home-made rink we were all proud of. It looked kind of nice in the soft glow of lights coming from the verandah.

I didn't own any skates, and I couldn't expect my parents to buy me a pair, so when my auntie told me she'd get me some I was overjoyed.

"Really! You would? Oh, thank you Auntie! Thank you!" My imagination took hold of me. "Could they be figure skates, like Barbara Ann Scott wore?" I already saw myself twirling on the ice, skating backwards, doing all kinds of loops and jumps, just like the world famous Olympic gold medallist.

"No, they can't," Auntie said firmly, "you'll slice your legs off on the sharp edges. The non-figure ones will have to do until you've learned to skate properly."

When the skates arrived I couldn't wait to put them on and get on the ice. A few children stood around and watched me lace up.

"They've got to be tighter than that."

"Remember to stay upright."

"Good luck on your first try!"

I stood up. The skates felt weird. I had trouble walking, slid all over the place, and fell over several times. Finally, I found myself at the edge of the rink.

To my surprise, one of the boys came over. It was Alex, an older boy who'd taken to walking with me to school on a regular basis and shielded my eyes from the crazy man who showed his privates to the children. The old man must have been desperate to hypnotize someone because he stood outside even in the cold of winter in just his old coat and boots.

"Would you like me to teach you how to skate?" Alex asked.

"Really? You'd do that?"

"Sure! I'd be glad to help you out."

Alex guided me gently onto the ice. He held my arm under the elbow and steered me round the rink, once, twice. "See? You've got the hang of it."

"Wow! Thanks."

"You've really never been on skates before?"

"Never."

"That's hard to believe. You're a natural!"

"You really think so?"

"Of course! This is way too easy for you! In fact, I think you're ready for something a little more challenging."

I looked around and coming at me were about eight children in a row, all holding hands.

"Grab onto the last boy in line, and start skating!" Alex told me. "He'll take care of you."

"Are you sure you know what you're doing?"

Alex smiled. "I know exactly what I'm doing."

As they were whipping by, the last boy reached out his hand to me. I managed to catch hold, and held on tight. I was on the end of the line, and felt myself being pulled faster and faster. It was thrilling.

Wow!

As we came out of a wide turn I must have been doing a hundred miles an hour. Suddenly, without warning, the boy holding my hand ever so tightly let go. I was moving like lightning, and the hand holding me disappeared!

I screamed.

Like a racecar over potholes I rattled over the bumpy ice. Too late, I realized nobody had taught me how to stop. I stumbled, went in circles, my legs going in two different directions at once. Down I went, landing on my chin. As I slid towards the end of the rink on my face I felt the skin coming off my nose and my cheeks. When I came to a stop, a bunch of children ran over. I could feel something warm on my face. Someone screamed. They thought I was dead. Irene took me to see the matron. She put ointments and bandages on my face, and the bleeding stopped.

They'd played 'crack the whip' on me. I'd scraped two inches of flesh off my face, my hands were raw and bleeding, but I'd done it! I'd survived my first skating lesson.

I also learned another lesson that day; trust no one. Especially Alex.

* * *

Soon the Christmas break arrived. We weren't allowed to go home for the holidays. I was told we'd be kept busy going to the gym, and skating. I wasn't sure I wanted to skate anymore.

The gymnasium on the dormitory grounds was in a huge building that was used year-round but particularly in winter. We had enough children to make up any number of teams for volleyball, basketball, and other sports. At these games we usually had an audience as well, as children not playing cheered on their friends.

In the dining room a huge Christmas tree was set up and decorated. I'd never seen such a big tree. Wrapped packages were placed under it, and we all wondered what was in them. I didn't know what to expect, because we'd never had a tree at home, except once when I was almost too young to remember. It didn't really matter, though. I would much rather have been at home, without a tree.

Our family always celebrated Christmas in the usual Doukhobor manner. We said prayers, and had a nice dinner in memory of Jesus Christ. No gifts or anything, just a spiritual celebration. Dad would play the guitar and we'd sing Christmas carols. We'd be happy because there'd be a feast mom had prepared, and to us Christmas was always about the family and the laughter.

Although our parents never gave us presents, my Auntie Vatkin sometimes brought something over. When I was about three years old I received a bridal doll. It wasn't wrapped, and it sat under the tiny tree in our little home. I treasured that doll. It was still at home with my family, and my sisters played with it. I only had one sister that Christmas, Kathrine, and I don't remember what she got. The next present I remember was a blue sports jacket with white piping. My sisters Kathrine and Marie also received the same gift. There was no tree; the jackets were wrapped in white tissue paper and placed on the coffee table. They were also a gift from my Auntie Vatkin. That was a year ago.

I felt a certain air of anticipation as Christmas approached, as I was interested to see how non-Doukhobors celebrated the holy day. What if they try and feed us turkey, I wondered, as the children at public school would be having? I wasn't allowed to eat turkey. None of us were. I knew what meat was because I'd helped my auntie cut bologna and bacon in her grocery store. It always smelled so good. Sometimes I'd be tempted to take a bite of the bologna, but I knew if I did I'd be in big trouble from my grandparents, and probably God too.

Christmas in the sanatorium turned out to be no big deal. The food was as bad as usual. The only difference was that Japanese oranges were on the tables. We were allowed to have one each. It tasted pretty good after the disappointing breakfast. Then the gifts were given out. Our names were called, and we went up to the front to collect. I got a little something, as did the others. It was a nice gesture, but I don't think any of us got a gift worthy of mention. The matrons tried to be cheerful, but I'm sure most of them would rather have been at home with their own families instead of standing guard over a bunch of religious fanatics' kids. We were all aware of the false smiles and good wishes for the season.

Christmas happened to fall on a visiting day that year. All the family came, and Mom brought extra good food for the holiday, too. I'd been looking forward to it, but it was hard for anyone to pretend it was a happy occasion. In fact, it was probably one of the most depressing Christmases of my life.

The tree looked really nice with all the decorations on it, but then the needles started to fall off, and it didn't look nice anymore.

7. MAKING FRIENDS
January – March, 1956

I couldn't stay away from the outdoor rink for long. I loved sports, and skating made me feel as free as a bird. I could forget everything as I glided around and around. As I practiced my beginner's jumps that first winter in New Denver, I had to admit Alex had been right about one thing - I was a natural. Sure, I fell over plenty of times, but pretty soon I was attempting everything I'd ever imagined on the ice. When winter storms blew too fiercely off the lake I'd spend long hours indoors caring for my skates, wiping down the moisture, making sure rust wouldn't develop on the blades. I polished them too, so they gleamed white. I even washed the laces; if I worked really hard, they too could look like new.

I was also beginning to feel a little more secure in my new home. Although I now knew I couldn't trust Alex without reliable supporting evidence, he still liked me, so the boys didn't pick on me the way they used to. Sophie too kept an eye out for me. And I was now good friends with some of the girls in the annex.

Irene and I had grown closer. She was just ten days older than me, and had a wonderful sense of humour. She was funny even when she was mad. She was the first person ever to tell me a dirty joke. I laughed until I cried, and repeated it to anyone who'd listen. She also knew a lot of swear words, and was teaching me new ones all the time. We shared secrets about our crushes on various boys, and our hope that we'd continue to be friends when the nightmare of New Denver came to an end.

Irene had interesting hair. In fact, she was one of the few girls whose hair was almost as bad as mine. Her bangs always stuck straight out, no matter what she did to them. She trimmed them herself sometimes, so she often had stray clippings of hair on her clothing. We offered to cut her bangs for her one time, but despite our best efforts they still stuck straight out, as usual. We wet them, and the same thing happened. Then someone told us that if we mixed hand soap with water the hair would stiffen in place. We tried that and it worked, except that her bangs hardened straight out, and she was royally angry with us.

She got her own back, though. One day the food looked so bad I didn't even bother tasting it. Irene however was eating it and, by all appearances, enjoying it. Anxious not to miss a rare treat, I shovelled a helping into my mouth - and gagged! I discovered she'd been chewing on nothing, and just sounded like she was having the meal of a lifetime. I couldn't help laughing, even though it was at my expense.

I never saw her cry, although there were times when her eyes were red and swollen. I envied her because she had her brother Eddie to look after her and keep her safe. I wondered if it was Eddie who was teaching her the swear words.

Roy's twin sister Anna and I became good friends. She was petite, with shiny, blonde hair. I wished mine could look like hers. We did in fact try to look like each other. We did our hair in the same style, and often dressed as if we were twins. Her laughter was contagious. I couldn't figure out how she chose me to be her friend, as she was beautiful and I was ugly and my teeth were crooked. Dad had told me to stick my thumb behind my teeth and pull outwards. I'd been doing that since before coming to New Denver, and now my teeth were slightly protruding. Maybe he'd meant me to push in. Anyway, Anna didn't seem to care about my appearance. We shared our secrets and our food supply. When we weren't in school we had free time, so we'd go skating together. We played cutouts, or sometimes we just wandered around town and looked in the windows.

Natalie also became my friend. She was tall, and very funny too. Anna, Natalie and I were always in each other's company. We were so close we were sometimes called the Three Musketeers, which made us smile. We'd go for long walks, or sit on the beach which was at our doorstep, wrapped up against the chill wind, and look out at the waves for hours, talking, laughing, even singing together.

I also became friends with Ruby. She was tall and skinny, and had naturally curly hair. She mimicked the matrons, and one of us had to be constantly on the lookout, because if we were caught we'd be in big trouble.

Alex was my first guy friend. He was three years older than me, but was still in the annex with the younger boys when I arrived in New Denver. It turned out that our parents had known each other for a long time, although I'd never met Alex before. Alex took me under his wing. Sophie was gentle and caring, but with Alex I had a protector at the top of the pecking order.

Alex was often kind to me, but also hard to understand. He took a great deal of pleasure in saying something, and then denying it completely. Who were we to argue? After all, he was one of the big boys. He'd often try to get me into trouble, too. He'd start something, and then walk away as if he didn't know anything about it. The stupid grin on his face always gave him away, though. He could be understanding and compassionate, yet at the same time he was full of pranks, always encouraging everyone to push the boundaries to see how much we could get away with. He was handsome, with dark hair, and I was glad he liked me. I kind of wanted him to be my boyfriend, but I was afraid of him.

As I made friends that first winter, I learned other children's stories of how they came to be there.

We were all in New Denver as wards of the Department of Child Welfare. Those who'd been in New Denver the longest had been sent there when their parents were sentenced to prison for taking part in the nude demonstration against enforced public schooling at Perry Siding. That had been in September of 1953, just over two years before I'd arrived. The violence the children described on that occasion was worse than I could imagine - police acted with incredible ferocity, clubbing and beating indiscriminately in a tent filled with unarmed men, women and children. Some of the children were traumatized from having seen their parents dragged away bleeding or unconscious, not knowing at the time whether they were alive or dead.

The stories from Krestova were just as horrific. In January of 1955 a force of seventy armed police officers had raided the settlement before dawn, taking children from their beds and savagely beating parents trying to keep their children from being taken away. I heard stories of police using pitchforks to poke into haystacks, officers crawling under homes with flashlights, searching for the elusive children. One boy's dog gave him away, wagging his tail at the boy hidden under the bed.

I didn't understand what was happening. It wasn't possible that a government could react in that way just because some parents didn't send their children to school. There had to be some other reason, something I wasn't being told. All my father ever said in response to my endless questioning was, 'You'll understand when you're older.' But it still made no sense. The best explanation my eight-year-old mind could come up with at the time was that the world had simply gone mad, and evil had taken over.

With the sudden arrival of the large numbers of children apprehended from Krestova, there had been severe overcrowding in the sanatorium. So when there was a flu outbreak a month later it spread like wildfire, and half the children were hospitalized. Construction of an annex was therefore ordered in the middle of 1955, some six months or so before I arrived, to combat the overcrowding. The main dormitory was separated into cubicles at the same time, for privacy.

Like me, most of the children had never been to school at all before coming to New Denver. At first, the director tried to have classes in the sanatorium building. Mr. Stickler, principal at the elementary school in town, offered to teach, but when he started classes that first winter the children refused to cooperate. Some stripped in protest and were carried in naked by law enforcement officers. But Mr. Stickler persevered, and by the following September about half of the children were ready to enroll in the public school in town. The other half remained in special classes in the sanatorium, either to bring their English up to scratch or because they were too old for their grade level.

* * *

From the moment of my arrival, life in New Denver was structured by rules and regulations. We ate breakfast, lunch and dinner at set times. We went to bed at a set time. We woke up, or rather we were woken up, at the same time every morning. Beds had to be made, clothes folded neatly. Our personal space had to be just so, all the time. The playroom had to be kept clean, the books and what few toys there were had to be put away. There was a place for everything, and everything had to be in its place. The rules were always there, and the matrons made sure we knew them. There was no such thing as 'I forgot', or 'I didn't know.' It seemed we were watched twenty-four hours a day, though we did get some time when we could slip off and go up the mountain or into town. I spoke Russian as often as I dared. When we were playing outside I hardly heard any English at all. But I was careful never to be caught speaking my mother tongue, so was never punished for it.

Discipline in the dormitory was much harsher than it was at school. In general, the public school teachers treated us no differently from the town children. Whenever they disciplined us it wasn't because we were Freedomites but because we'd done something wrong. I was an average student, although I thought I was smarter because I spoke two languages and could read and write. I remember some of the children getting yelled at because they couldn't speak English. When I tried to help them, some accepted my help gratefully while others stubbornly wanted to be left alone.

Among the pupils there was a mixture of culture, heritage, colour, religion and languages, so it's not surprising there was some teasing in school. 'Dirty Douk' was a common taunt. However, overall, the children got along well with each other. I heard that when the dormitory first opened, a lot of people in New Denver were very apprehensive about having children of Freedomites coming to their town. Our history of bombings, burnings and public displays of nudity made many uncomfortable. The town children were cautious as well, but we soon settled into a peaceful coexistence.

One of the girls in my class who was always very friendly was Suzy Hashimoto. Although she was Japanese and I was European, I thought we looked like twins. Her haircut was as bad as mine, and it seemed we had the same ugly green dress. We skipped at school, and played marbles during recess and lunch hour. Suzy told me one of her relatives had owned a hotel in Vancouver, but that then they lost everything and her family had to move to New Denver.

The first visiting day in February was bitterly cold. I was glad I no longer cried, or I was sure my tears would have frozen on my cheeks. Only my mom and dad and Auntie Vatkin were there. My sisters hadn't come, and I missed them terribly. We all huddled on a blanket as I ate the wonderful food that was brought for me. My mother was crying, and I watched to see if her tears would freeze. The warmth of my family was like food for my soul, but all I had after they left was the memory.

That night I heard girls whimpering after lights out. The matron just yelled at them to shut up.

Into the bleakest part of my first winter in New Denver came Valentine's Day. Miss Spencer brought in heart-shaped cookies with icing and sparkles, and we each had an envelope attached to our desk for cards. The girls all talked about their boyfriends. I didn't have one, but I wasn't sure I needed one anyway. The boys got really jealous if their girlfriends talked to other boys.

That's not to say I didn't think about boys. Alex still walked me to school on occasion, but I already knew I couldn't trust him. Then there was Eugene. Eugene was handsome, but he was a show-off, and always getting in trouble, too. All the girls thought Eugene was wonderful because he was so tall and strutted around. He had an arrogance to him that the girls liked. I preferred Theo. He was my friend, and really smart. When the girls talked about Theo we all said he'd be a scientist, or something brainy like that. He talked very fast, and we had to listen carefully or we missed what he was saying. The teachers liked Theo too, because he always got high marks on his work.

But Carl was the cutest. He was in grade one with me at school, and he had nice freckles. He sometimes held the door open for me in class. He was such a gentleman, just like in the movies. I wanted Carl to be my boyfriend, but he was shy and didn't even look at me when I talked to him, so I guessed that would never happen. I wanted to kiss Carl once, but I was afraid to, even on the cheek, because the other children would just give us both trouble. I figured I could always kiss him later, when I was older.

On Saturday nights, though not every Saturday, the playroom in the annex became the movie theatre. I loved movie night, because I could escape my surroundings for as long as the movie played. We all got a big laugh from the cartoons, and thought it very mature of us to be able to choose the movie to be shown next.

For days afterwards, our playtime activities would be inspired by whatever film we'd just seen. Irene and I especially loved acting out scenes of passion and high drama as a prince and princess from medieval times, but death, murder and cruelty scenes were popular too. I also enjoyed playing cowboys and Indians, for by now I'd seen enough western movies that the gunfights didn't bother me anymore. I'm sure my family would have been aghast if they'd known I took pleasure in pretending to shoot people to death.

I was usually the cowboy, and Irene would get angry with me.

"Why are you the good guy all the time?" she'd protest.

I had a perfectly logical explanation. "I have to be the cowboy," I patiently explained, "because I've got a cowboy hat."

My auntie had bought me a red felt cowboy hat fringed with tiny toys all the way around. I had the hat, and I wasn't about to share it with her. I never shared my hat with anyone, except on the odd occasion someone wanted to wear it for a photograph. And until she got her own hat I'd be the cowboy and she'd continue to be the Indian.

"Besides, you make a better Indian than I would." Irene had told a group of us that her brother Eddie had magical powers. He knew an Indian chief, and that chief had taught Eddie how to walk on water. It only happened in the summertime when there was a full moon. I couldn't wait to be old enough to sleep in the main dormitory, so that at night I could watch Eddie perform his trick of walking on the lake. "If I had a brother like that I sure wouldn't want to be the cowboy."

"If that's so, then why do you get to be the princess all the time?" Irene demanded.

"Simple," I replied. "I look more like a princess than you do!"

One of the many westerns we watched was called 'Hellfire.' It had a female lead called Doll Brown. She was supposed to be a good gunwoman, though she did shoot her husband. She had steely eyes, and didn't let anyone push her around. For weeks afterwards I believed that if I could twirl and holster a revolver like she did while flashing a no-nonsense glare, people wouldn't push me around either. I was an adult before I realized it only works when you have real bullets in the gun.

My work in school was good, and I was quick to put my hand up whenever the teacher asked a question. But I realized very shortly after arriving that even if I could follow the action on a movie screen, my eyesight wasn't strong enough to read the chalkboard from where I was sitting at the back of the room. I discovered though that if I squinted I could more easily make out whatever was written on the board. Soon I became adept at pulling both eyes with one hand and then quickly writing with the other hand.

"Stupid can't see!" some of the kids chanted.

Well, I either look stupid, or stay stupid, I thought. I didn't really care anyway. With my ugly haircut I already looked stupid, so who cared if I looked like I was trying to squeeze my eyeballs out of their sockets.

On the other hand, it occurred to me that if with all the tugging and pulling I was doing my eyes became as slanted as those of my Japanese schoolmates, my parents might not recognize me the next time they came to visit. So I told the teacher, and she arranged to have my eyes examined. The school nurse checked me out and told me there was nothing wrong with my eyesight.

Except that I still couldn't see.

When I told the teacher, she moved me to the front of the class. I didn't want to be at the front. I knew I'd get into trouble there, because I liked to fool around. I'd rather have stayed at the back where the teacher couldn't see us passing notes or sharing candy and gum, because that was way more fun. I had to be careful when I chewed gum because I liked to blow bubbles and make the gum snap.

Lena, one of the girls from the annex, was given a pair of glasses. She claimed to be quite surprised as she could see perfectly well.

"Maybe our results got mixed up and you've received my glasses," I suggested.

"Could be. I certainly don't need them."

"In that case, maybe I could borrow them sometimes. If you're not using them."

"Perhaps."

"Could I borrow them now? Just to see if they help?"

"I don't know, though. I think I might just hang on to them."

"But you said you don't need them!"

"Well, you never know..."

Pretty soon I'd perfected my New Denver Squint. I held the paper firmly on the desk with my left elbow, a pencil in my right hand. Then I shut my right eye, and pulled at my left eye with my left hand. It was an uncomfortable angle for writing, but at least I could make out the words on the board. If I hadn't sat at the front of the class I wouldn't have been able to read a thing.

Sometimes I tried really hard to be a good student because I wanted my parents to be proud of me. Sometimes I didn't care about anything at all, except that I wanted to go home.

Individuality wasn't encouraged in the dorms. We were all issued the same blue melton cloth jackets with white piping down the sleeves, and the same heavy denim jeans. Our jeans were way too long, so we used to roll them up a couple of times, which made the bottoms really bulky. The only way to tell each person's clothing apart was by the numbers embroidered inside. I really believe the idea was to make us all look alike, in the hope we'd all end up thinking alike.

We were allowed to wear clothing from home though, if we had any. I was one of the children who possessed a fair amount, as my mother was a great seamstress who could make anything she wanted to, and in next to no time, too. She took great pride in sewing for her family. I know she'd much rather have embroidered my name instead of a number on my clothing.

Laundry day was once a week. I didn't like that, because my jeans held the stench of the food I'd been eating for days. At first I could barely keep from gagging as I pulled them on, but after a while I just got used to the smell. We were responsible for our own clothing, and had to see that it went in the right bin for the laundry. Anything that was left out we had to wash ourselves.

We also had to iron anything we wanted ourselves, as it wasn't done for us. Our ironing board was made for grown-ups, and so it was an effort for us to reach the top. We used to stack books, or find old wooden boxes to use as stepstools. I burned holes in some of the things I tried to iron. Sometimes we'd have to do ironing for the other dormitories. My heart would be pounding as I tried my utmost not to burn anything, for if that happened the wrath of the matron would be on us. At times like that the older girls were great. They were usually helpful, and would show us youngsters the best way to do things.

It didn't matter what it was I was learning though, my heart was always in my mouth. Most of my days were spent looking over my shoulder, as the fear of doing something wrong, and then of being caught and punished, was enough to make me want to throw up.

I was playing outside after getting back from school one day when someone approached me.

"Mrs. Norton wants to see you."

"What for?"

"Don't know. But it's the third time she's called you."

I couldn't guess what it might be about, but as I walked into the annex I knew right away I was in trouble. Mrs. Norton was waiting for me by the office.

"I found these," she said, holding up a pair of jeans. She had a more-than-usually sour look on her face. "Why were they not put in the wash?"

I always paid careful attention to the rules, but somehow I'd overlooked a pair of jeans that laundry day. I guessed Matron had checked our lockers, discovered my jeans, and then lain in wait for me.

"Well?"

"I forgot."

"You forgot?" Her tone was dry and unimpressed. Fear gripped me. Please, not the strap! I'd heard about her strappings.

"How do you know they're mine?" I blurted out. I hoped to demolish the case against me by throwing doubt on her sole item of incriminating evidence, but as soon as I'd spoken I realized my mistake. Mrs. Norton showed me the number eighty-five, very visible on the inside of the waistband.

"I thought they'd be fine for another week," I protested.

"They're not fine. They're filthy! And irresponsible children like you must learn to pay attention to the rules."

Oh God, I knew it. I was going to get the strap! My heart pounded like crazy. Already my wrists were hurting.

"I apologize about my oversight regarding the jeans, Mrs. Norton," I stammered, trying to appeal to her better nature. "In fact, I was just about to wash them anyway, right now. So if I could just..."

"Put out your hands."

Down came the strap. It felt like I'd got into nettles, and a million mosquitoes and bees were stinging me. She hit me once on each wrist. I thought I was going to faint. I couldn't believe how much it hurt. Then she did it again. My wrists were on fire. Little blood blisters were already forming. I was screaming inside, but my face showed nothing.

"Now take these dirty jeans and wash them!"

I walked outside to where some of my friends had gathered.

"How was it?"

My arms were throbbing to my fingertips, and each throb was an explosion of pain.

"Fuck, that hurt," I said casually.

I'd started using that awful swear word, knowing my mom would faint if she heard me. I was learning all the time how to be tough. And even better, how to sound tough. We all learned how to swear, and I certainly used the best words I knew to describe the hurt I felt on my wrist. That 'F' word really helped.

"Yeah, she's a bitch, that one."

I thought I'd just go across to the laundry and pop them through. No such luck. I had to wash them by hand, which was a punishment almost worse than the first. The only sink available to me was in the pink room, next to the playroom in the annex. Putting my raw skin into the hot wash water was agony. Once I got the jeans wet they were so heavy I could barely lift them. No matter how much I scrubbed, it didn't seem to make any difference. I struggled for a long time, rubbing by hand, putting on a little soap, rubbing some more, then endlessly trying to rinse the soap out with clear water. My arms were aching. Some of the blood blisters had burst, and the sting of soap in my wounds finally brought me to tears. It hurt like hell, and no one cared.

By then I'd developed a game in which I'd imagine myself far, far away. I kept scrubbing and rinsing, but at the same time I was somewhere else, perhaps eating a dark chocolate ice cream cone. I could taste the coolness of the cone, and feel the velvety chocolate on my tongue - until all of a sudden reality reasserted itself, and I was brought back again to the hell of New Denver.

There was no way I could wring the jeans out on my own, so I had to ask Anna to help me. Even then, I could barely carry them as we took them outside to hang them up to dry on a makeshift clothesline.

That night as I picked at my burned and wrinkled skin I decided that was the last time I was putting myself through such torture. When I was grown up I'd buy an automatic washing machine. For the moment, though, I had to find a scrubbing board.

* * *

Throughout my time in New Denver I wrote many, many letters home. Generally I wrote to both parents at once, but as I was closer to my mother I addressed myself more to her. I also wrote to my sisters, to my auntie, and to my grandparents. I didn't know until many years later that my grandmother couldn't read or write. Because I didn't want my mom to worry about me I'd try and tell her good news, about the food, about school and the things I'd learned, and then tell her about what some of the other children were doing as well. In hindsight, I probably wrote the same thing over and over, just wording it differently.

Letters from home were like Christmas. Often my mom would send a parcel containing cookies or candies, or sometimes an item of clothing, but the best part was always the letter. My heart filled with joy as I read about the small and insignificant events of family life. Mom's letters unfolded like movies in my mind, and reading them I could picture Kathrine and Marie helping her with the baking or the gardening, and I could escape the reality of where I was. The crash that came when I finished reading was painful. I was aware only of an overwhelming desire to go home and be a part of my family again. Sometimes the sadness would last until the next letter came. I loved to hear from my little sisters. They were learning to read and write fairly well. But the best letters were always from my mom. I missed her more than anyone, and cried silently for her most nights.

* * *

Weeks went by. The food was still awful, and the gnawing hunger that was a constant part of life in New Denver never let up.

Our parents usually gave us food when they came to visit, but since we weren't allowed to keep anything perishable in our lockers we had to eat it all the same day. Sometimes they'd give us a little money so we could buy candy at the grocery store on the way into town. The store was run by a Japanese man called Taro, who also worked in the laundry at the sanatorium. Boy, I was glad I didn't have that job. Imagine having to do laundry for a hundred or more children! We liked going to Taro's store because he was so friendly, and the candy there was really good.

Sometimes too, if we didn't have enough money, Taro would throw in an extra candy so we could all have a taste. One of my favourites was graham wafer crackers with sugar and cinnamon on them. The package was fairly large, and way too much for a child. I'd eat as much as I possibly could without puking, and then share the rest.

He also sold a candy wrapped in paper that was hard to peel off.

"Don't worry about that," Taro said to me. "You can just eat it, paper and all!"

"Are you sure?" My auntie's store in Grand Forks had all sorts of candy, and I'd never heard of that before. And I'd certainly tried every kind she had.

"Sure I'm sure!" He popped one in his mouth and smiled to show me it was okay.

They were called 'white rabbit' candies. Taro told us the paper was made from rice, and that they came from Japan. I tried one too. It tasted strange at first, but also special. It was as if I'd been initiated into a secret ritual unknown to the outside world. Besides, it seemed I got more when I ate the paper.

From then on, my hope on visiting days was that my parents would give me money so I could go to Taro's store and pig out on white rabbits. I'd buy a bag and do the same thing I'd done with the graham wafers - eat, eat, eat - and then share the rest. The other children yelled 'hunks!' when they wanted a taste of what someone was eating. White rabbits were a 'no hunks!' treat.

My friend Ruby and I came up with a scheme to raise a little extra money whenever our food resources were getting low. Giggling, we'd wrap bandanas around our faces so that only our eyes were showing, and run over to the guard shack. We'd take out our long-tailed combs and pretend they were pistols. Then, putting on our best steely-eyed Doll Brown look, we'd tell Tadi it was a stick-up. Sometimes we blocked the guard shack door with a piece of wood and told him he'd stay in there until he came up with a ransom. He'd cheerfully pass a couple of nickels through the window and we'd unblock the door. We'd rush away before pulling off our bandanas, hoping he hadn't recognized us.

We did this at least once a week, but only when Tadi was on duty. I don't know if any of the other children did it, and we certainly weren't going to tell, because Tadi was a gold mine to us. Tadi was by far the nicest person I met in New Denver, and not just because he gave us nickels. He had sad eyes though, and sometimes they had tears in them. Tadi was always kind to us, and Taro allowed us to poke around his store for as long as we liked. I thought Taro and Tadi had to be related, because they were both so friendly.

It was nice to have adults who treated us like regular people. When we went into other stores the clerks never took their eyes off us. We just wanted to buy cookies or candies, but they thought we were all really bad kids.

I couldn't really blame them. New Denver must have been a quiet town until the dormitory opened and the school suddenly filled up with strange children. On visiting days there were crowds of people from outside, many of whom only spoke Russian, and sometimes tempers would flare. Everything was so different from the way it was before. Their little town was no longer a quiet place to live.

8. THE FEARSOME MISS CREWELL
Spring, 1956

In early April of 1956, some four months after my arrival, control of the sanatorium passed from the Department of Child Welfare to the local school district. To mark the handover, its official name was changed to the New Denver Elementary School Dormitory. Unofficially, the 'San' now became the 'Dorm'. Mr. Stickler, the principal at the elementary school in town who'd been giving classes in the sanatorium, now took over as the dorm's new director. He discharged the entire supervisory staff and recruited a new nurse/matron, as well as a recreational director whose task appeared to be to keep us busy in the gym when we weren't otherwise occupied.

John Stickler was a slight man, with dark, somewhat curly hair. His lip too curled, so that he talked almost out of the side of his mouth. He spoke a little fast, and with a slight stutter. His initials were J. A., which we immediately claimed stood for Jackass. He carried himself like a cocky little rooster, both at the dorm and at the school, where he remained the principal. The previous director of the dormitory had been fairly quiet. I'd hardly ever seen him, and was quite happy not to. Mr. Stickler however enjoyed being the boss. He was strict, very mean, and was always punishing someone or other. He and his wife lived in a house immediately beside the dorms. They had two girls, Elaine and Brenda, and a little boy, William. The girls didn't really bother with us, but we all sure liked the little boy. He was so cute.

Our new matron was Miss Crewell. She was huge, starchier even than Mrs. Norton but without the glamorous nails and perm, and made a weird breathing noise that earned her the nickname of 'the Hisser'. We soon came to recognize when she was hovering behind one of us, watching for the mistake that would give her an excuse to inflict herself on us. She moved into the staff apartment in the annex. I wanted to live in an apartment like that when I got older, but I sure hoped I wouldn't end up looking like Miss Crewell. I was ugly enough already.

Miss Crewell was the meanest person in the world. I feared her more than anyone. Just the sound of her footsteps was enough to make my heart pound. Her snake's-hiss breathing, which put everyone on guard against a sudden unexpected strike from nowhere, remains etched in my mind. I presume it was because she was so fat that she made her weird breathing noise, and also because of her weight that her shoes cried out when she walked. The only good thing was that when we were being naughty after lights out we could sometimes hear a soft, warning hiss, or the sound of her shoes squeaking on the floor as she tiptoed towards the doorway hoping to catch us unawares.

The janitors too were let go, and from that point on we, the children, became the work force in the dormitories. Rosters were posted with chores listed for each child. Everyday tasks included helping in the kitchen and washing up, while every Saturday we now had to clean the entire buildings, including the director's home and the matron's apartment, and do yard work. We were the ones who kept the bathrooms scrubbed, the windows washed, the floors swept, mopped and polished. When washing windows we had to climb on ladders to reach the topmost panes, which scared me because I was afraid of heights. I hated cleaning the bathrooms, especially the boys' side. The boys would pee on the walls just to be stupid, and the stink was horrible. I'd never cleaned a flush toilet or a shower stall before, because at home we had an outdoor toilet and a galvanized tub. Many of the other girls didn't know how to clean them either, but together we worked it out. We were always watched, to make sure all work was done to their exacting standards. I tried to pretend I was on an adventure, and that this was part of it. We worked and we worked and we worked.

The annex was a fairly large building - the boys' and girls' sleeping areas, the playroom, the large pink room that doubled as a sick bay and storage room, the bathrooms, the office and Matron's apartment - and every inch had to be swept. Then, when we were done sweeping, the floors had to be washed. They were linoleum, but it was hard because of the mops we were given to use. It took all my strength just to wring out what water I could into the bucket, and then lift the still-sopping mop onto the floor. Sometimes it took two of us to swing one mop.

When the floor was dry it had to be polished using a huge electric floor polisher, which was way too big to be operated by one child. Needless to say, none of us had ever handled anything like it. The first time we used it, Matron took three girls and showed them how it worked, then left the room. When I looked in later I saw one child holding the controls and steering, with the other two balanced on the front end where the brushes were, shrieking and hanging on for dear life.

When we cleaned Miss Crewell's apartment we had to be careful to make everything look nice. If we dusted under anything we had to put it back exactly as we'd found it; nothing could be left out of place. Sometimes we had to iron Miss Crewell's clothes as well. I was always worried I'd put a big burn patch on one of her blouses. Lord only knows what kind of trouble a child could get into for doing that. The only good thing about cleaning her apartment was getting to play with her cat. Oh, how we all loved that cat! It was the only pet on the property we were allowed to touch. That poor cat used to run away from us when we walked into Matron's quarters, not because we were mean to it but because of all the noise we made while cleaning.

Some of the bigger children had to help in the on-site laundry, but I never worked there because I was too small to be able to reach all the equipment. Children also had to maintain the gymnasium and all its equipment, and I never worked there, either. The floor was polished until you could see your face in it, and not a cobweb could be seen anywhere. The equipment room was so neat you'd think elves came in and tidied up while we slept. In fact, the children did all the work.

More children were continually being brought to the dormitory during the time I was there. That spring a new girl called Connie Stuchnoff arrived at the annex. She had a great sense of humour, and I took an immediate liking to her.

"They gave me the number fifty-eight," she said.

"Really? You're fifty-eight? But I'm eighty-five!"

"So?"

"So fifty-eight is eighty-five backwards!" I said. "There's a connection already! Maybe we're meant to be friends!"

"Perhaps... but it might be an upside down, sideways sort of friendship..."

Connie was very pretty, with nice teeth. Her hair was beautiful, and hung in long, thick braids. Miss Crewell didn't cut them, which annoyed me because

Mrs. Norton had sure hacked mine. I wondered why the other children hadn't thought she was a spy as they had with me.

"I'm from Krestova." she explained. "They already know me. In fact, I'm one of the last children from there who's not already in New Denver."

"How come the police didn't find you when they did the big round-up?"

"I was in the forest at the time," she said. "I'd been hiding there since I was six." She said her mom packed her a lunch every day. The way she described it made my mouth water.

"You must've liked the forest much better than here," I said.

"Not really. It was a very hard life."

As we talked we discovered that my dad and her mom had known each other from when they were little, and that our parents were still very good friends. In fact, during the rest of my time in New Denver they often came in together on visiting days. As I was one of the first girls to befriend Connie, I took it on myself to show her around and to fill her in on the rules, both official and unspoken. I guess I didn't do such a good job, as she was in trouble pretty much on a daily basis, in school and at the dorm.

Although so often in trouble, Connie learned quickly not to show emotion to the matrons. Most of us picked up on that one right away. When we showed emotion of any sort we were laying ourselves bare. If we were stone-faced and uncaring we blended into the woodwork and were left alone. One day Miss Crewell caught Connie crying. She was just lonely for her family, that's all. Matron took her into the office and gave her the strap, and told her crying wasn't allowed. I never saw Connie cry again.

She also gave the appearance of being indifferent to the world around her. When questioned about anything by the matrons, Connie would feign ignorance, pretend she couldn't understand, or merely walk away, which would warrant another strapping. Many times when I spoke to her the reply would be 'Huh?' I'd have to repeat everything I'd said, and once again all I'd get was 'Huh?' It was frustrating, but at the same time I envied her ability to retreat so easily into her own world. She tried to teach me how to hold my feelings deep inside and appear on the surface to be different from how I was feeling. I tried hard to master the technique, but never managed it as successfully as she did. Connie was never afraid to offer an opinion, whatever the topic. She was stubborn, and could argue that black was white, just for the sake of it. Often she'd get quite fierce, but never backed down from anyone. She was so tough some of the boys were afraid of her. I admired her, and I was glad she was my friend, but I knew I could never be brave like her. She was smart, too. She taught me how to pretend to swallow pills, and then spit them out when Matron wasn't watching. She was also a happy child. Well, as happy as anyone can be in a residential setting. Her sense of humour was unparalleled. Things that didn't appear in the least bit humorous would bring gales of laughter from her. Many times over my years in the dorm she was a ray of sunshine to me, and our friendship continues to this day.

* * *

School was great and I loved to learn, but I was also looking forward to going home for the spring break. I hadn't thought much about the break until then, but as the school term neared its end it was on my mind day and night. Nobody said anything about it, though. So finally I asked a friend when we got to go home.

"Never," was the short reply.

"What? You mean we don't get to go home till summer?"

"We don't get to go home ever! We're here until we turn fifteen or our parents agree to send us to public school."

"What!!!" I couldn't believe it. I'd been dreaming about running in the garden with Kathrine and Marie, laughing and playing together for a brief respite before returning to our little prison.

"But school's out," I said. "So what are we going to do on break, then?"

One of the first things the director had us do was strip all the wax off the floors in the annex. There was the boys' section, the girls' section, the playroom, the sick room, the bathrooms, the office, and lastly, the private quarters of Miss Crewell. It took days to do them all.

Then we had to rewax and polish them, and that was when the fun began. I was sent to get the electric floor polisher from the pink room. It was almost taller than I was and way too heavy for one person to move alone, so I called to Ruby and Irene for help. Together we managed to drag it into the playroom. Irene offered to show me how it worked.

"It's easy," she said. "Just flip that switch, then hold the handles tight while I plug it in. And whatever you do, don't let go!"

As she pushed the plug into the outlet, the polisher suddenly jerked into life and shot off across the floor with a whine like a jet engine, dragging me behind it. I squealed in panic. My instinct was to cling to the handles and try to wrestle the monster to the floor before it crashed through the far wall. It was hopeless, but I didn't know what else to do. Visions flashed through my imagination in swift succession: papers flying as the polisher ploughed relentlessly through the office walls; matron's cat, startled by the explosion of glass and splintered wood, trying in vain to flee; a stern-faced director solemnly reprimanding me in front of the whole dormitory for destroying matron's apartment with a floor polisher, 'Never in all my years...' I sobbed a silent prayer as the moment of impact approached. *Please God, not her lovely cat!*

Suddenly the polisher stopped, just feet from the wall. I clung to the handles, limp with exhaustion and disbelief, not quite sure how the strange miracle had happened, but glad that it had. I was brought out of my trance by the sound of Ruby and Irene splitting their sides with laughter.

"What a scream!"

"You should have seen your face!"

"What happened?" I asked. "Why did it stop?"

Irene pointed behind me. The electrical cord had been pulled out of the wall by the polisher when it had reached the limit of its travel.

"I never thought we'd get you with that one!"

I couldn't believe it. I'd been had yet again.

"Come on," Irene said, "we'll show you how it's done."

I hesitated. "You're kidding, right?"

"We'll do it properly this time. We promise!"

I didn't see I had much choice. "Okay. So how does it work?"

Irene showed me the controls while Ruby plugged it in again. Then they both went round the front and climbed onto the head of the polisher.

"What are you doing up there?"

"We have to weigh it down, otherwise... well, you've already seen what'd happen."

This time I braced myself before the on switch was hit. The polisher roared into life, then surged forward, but the two girls on the front provided enough ballast to keep it from getting totally out of control. I needed help to steer for a while, but soon got the hang of it. After a time we switched over, and Irene and I stood on the front end while Ruby steered.

Then it was Irene's turn to steer. Standing on the brush end with Ruby I saw the chance to get my own back.

"Now!" I whispered.

We both jumped off at the same time, and instantly the polisher went crazy. Now it was Irene's turn to squeal, but this time it was with delight. She treated it like a fairground ride, and what a ride it was! All three of us screamed with laughter as the machine weaved its way around the playroom floor, dragging Irene behind it.

9. A PLACE OF OUR OWN

Spring, 1956

Our time was mostly occupied by school, work around the dorms, and activities in the gym. There was always someone telling us what to do, how to do it, when to eat, sleep, shower, play. As I grew accustomed to the rules and regulations, life became somewhat easier. The fear never left though, and I was constantly on the lookout for approaching caregivers. It didn't take much to get them wound up and on the warpath with us. Then punishment was handed out as easily as my auntie used to give out candy.

We were used to being bossed around all the time, but, boy, did we ever take it out on those who were weaker than we were! Even some of the children at public school were afraid of us.

I'd wanted to be a lady when I grew up, but I guessed I wouldn't be able to do that any more. It wasn't really so bad though, because instead it meant I could climb trees, and jump down onto the gravel below. I was pretty tough. I didn't cry when I'd sprain an arm, or twist an ankle. It might hurt for a couple of days, but one of the other girls always brushed my hair for me, or helped me pull on my socks, so the matrons wouldn't know.

I could run really fast too. That was a good thing, because sometimes we made the older boys really mad at us, and we had to run for our lives from them.

By now I could cover my emotions almost to perfection, and my face rarely registered anything. I felt like a zombie sometimes, but I had a strong will to survive, and inside my head the wheels were always turning as I planned all the things I needed to learn better so I could show even less emotion. Quite an undertaking for an eight year old, but I wasn't alone. We were all in the same boat: afraid of the matrons, and even worse, afraid of each other.

After visiting hour we'd always gather around and share what snacks we had from our parents. My aunt often gave me a little pocket money, and it didn't take long for me to round up some friends and head over to Taro's store, where we'd promptly spend all of it. The next visiting day someone else would receive money, and again a gang of us would get together and head for the store. Even though we were always hungry, we shared.

One day a group of us got together and decided we needed a place of our own, where we could hide things away from the prying eyes of the matrons. We all had treasures; things we'd found on the way to school, or while wandering the back lanes of the town. It could be a pretty rock, a chain, a few marbles. And we urgently needed somewhere to store the surplus food our parents brought that we couldn't finish during visiting hour. It had always been forbidden to store food in our lockers, but the new director was determined to enforce this law rigidly. Anything that turned up in a locker search that the matrons deemed unauthorized was liable to be confiscated.

So we decided to build a fort.

The spot we chose was high on the side of the mountain that loomed over the dorm. As we set off we picked up broken branches, armfuls of ferns, and anything else we thought might be useful. We found a large forked branch at the bottom of the mountain that looked just right. Three of us dragged it all the way up to the well-hidden spot we'd selected under the shelter of a huge tree.

The boys had a secret hideout too. It was a tree-house down by the lake, behind Stickler's house. You had to look hard to find it, but once you knew where it was it was easy to get to. We were afraid of the boys so we never went near their place. Ours would be harder to get to, and very well hidden. Even so, we posted look-outs; we feared that if the boys ever discovered our secret place they'd wreck it and steal everything we'd hidden there.

There were half a dozen of us involved. We worked hard, and after hours of hauling all kinds of fallen wood into place our hideout was finished. It was pretty small inside - about six feet across and three feet tall - but there was enough room to store food, and for a couple of girls to crawl inside and stretch out. And it was dry. We'd chosen branches with lots of foliage on them for the outside, and we lined the floor of our secret place with layers of ferns, dry grass and leaves.

My, we were a proud lot! We stole an old blanket to spread out on the floor. Then we found cardboard boxes, printed our names on them, and left them inside the fort, ready to be filled with food. We hurried down the mountain to Taro's store to spend everything we had on cookies, soft drinks and candy, then returned to stash our goodies in the appropriate boxes.

We felt pretty smug, knowing that over the following week we'd be able to stop by whenever we wanted and stuff our faces with the delights stored in our secret hideaway.

Well, the tomorrows of feasting never came. We hurried to our fort after school the next day and discovered to our dismay that animals had got into everything. The fort was ripped apart and the cardboard boxes scattered all over. I wanted to cry. All that we'd worked so hard to build was ruined. It also meant that when we bought goodies we'd have to go back to sharing or else eating till we puked.

Life was strange. Either we were starving because the food was so bad, or we filled ourselves with junk food and got on a sugar high, and then wanted to throw up because our tummies were so upset. We rebuilt the fort, but then the boys found us, so it was no longer a secret. We decided not to use the hideout as a food store because even if the animals didn't come back the boys would just eat it all anyway. I liked to go and sit in there sometimes. It was good to have a place we could use for girl talk, and as an escape from the annex. Once four of us jammed in there and told scary stories to each other while it rained.

I never went to the boys' secret place, even when Alex said he'd show it to me. I heard that one of the older boys once kissed one of the older girls in there. I didn't trust the boys because they were always laughing at us and criticized everything about us. There was no way I was going inside their fort. I didn't want to kiss anyone.

We had a community nurse who came by the school to give us shots. She wore a blue skirt with a matching jacket, and had salt-and-pepper hair which curled from under her white nurse's hat. On the pocket of the jacket was a brooch-like pin with gold trim. She smelled really clean, and her hair was in tight rings. I wondered if it was natural. She laid out her needles and cotton batting on Miss Spencer's desk, and we were called up in alphabetical order.

The needle was enormous. I thought it would go right through my bones and out the other side. But the nurse didn't listen when I tried to explain my concern. Instead she just told me to roll up my sleeve. She grabbed my arm, and slowly plunged the needle into my flesh.

"Oww!" I thought she was trying to kill me.

"What's the matter?"

"It hurts!"

"Don't be such a baby."

I was so nervous my whole body went rigid, which only made it all the more difficult, for both of us. The nurse didn't try to comfort me in any way. Instead she just kept pushing the needle in. I wondered if regular nurses were all as mean as her.

As soon as the needle came out I pretended I had to pee. I ran to the bathroom and locked myself in the stall so no one could see me crying. Then I dried my tears, and returned to class. I knew if the other children saw me crying I'd get teased badly, or maybe even beaten up. Anyone who cried was a sissy, and deserved to cry even more. I didn't share my pain or my fears with the other children. I wasn't a sissy.

We were also taken to the dentist in New Denver a couple of times a year. That was another nightmare for us. The dentist was even worse than the nurse. His office harboured a strange smell of damp cabbage, the source of which I was never able to trace with any confidence. My best guess was that it came from the antique chair he made us sit in, which looked as if it came from the dump. It creaked when he raised it up, and the filling, which spilled out in odd places, made me sneeze.

The first time I was taken to him I had no idea what to expect. I believed my teeth were perfect, because my mom always made sure I looked after them. I climbed into the chair and smiled, assuming he'd be kind and gentle. He reached into my mouth and started to floss my teeth with what felt like wire. I moaned softly.

"What's the problem?" he grunted.

"It hurts."

"Don't be such a crybaby!"

He prodded in my mouth with a round mirror on a stick, told me I had lots of cavities, and proceeded to freeze my gums. When he gave the needle it hurt even more than when the school nurse did it. The pain was unbearable, and I started to cry. He rolled his eyes in frustration. I wondered if he and the nurse were related, or maybe went to the same mean school. When he drilled a cavity I got a sharp, hot pain in that tooth, but he wouldn't let me tell him. I gripped the arms of the chair, tensing my body in strange contortions to avoid shrieking with pain, and he just give me a dirty look. He drilled and filled, and then told me I was done. I was happy to be out of there.

The older girls said he wasn't too bad. Maybe he was nicer to them. He sure hated us younger ones. I didn't like that he talked so much to his assistant instead of paying attention to what he was doing.

From then on I tried hard to brush my teeth properly because I hated going to see him. It didn't seem to make any difference though, because I always had to have fillings, and a lot of my teeth were pulled. I couldn't believe the amount of work he did each time I went to him. And each time I got the same rough treatment as before. I decided I'd get false teeth when I got home, because I sure didn't like the pain of real ones. The experience gave me a strong aversion to dentists, and it was a long time before I'd agree to see one after my release from New Denver.

Strapping was pretty much an everyday occurrence, and avoiding it meant getting to know the enemy's strengths and weaknesses and exploiting them to the full. It was psychological warfare, and we very quickly learned how to modify our behaviour to suit the temperament of whichever matron was on duty at the time.

Miss Crewell was the worst. When she patrolled the bedroom at night we didn't have to imagine monsters. There was a real live one right there beside us. One night one of the girls was weeping after we'd all gone to bed. An older girl climbed into bed with her to try and comfort her.

"Hush. It's okay," she said. "It'll be all right, you'll see."

Suddenly we heard the creaking steps of Miss Crewell as she checked on us. When she came on the two girls she pulled both of them out of bed and marched them to the office. We could hear the whoosh and the crack of the razor strap as it came down on their outstretched hands. After they returned to bed we lay awake listening for the sounds of sobbing, but that never happened. I guess those two knew enough not to cry. We might cry for our families, but hardly anyone there ever cried after a strapping. We were tough little girls, and the bitch matrons wouldn't see anyone cry, not today, not ever. We were always talking about how we were going to beat the hell out of the matrons when we grew up.

Mrs. Black was sometimes nice. She was a tall lady, and her hair was permed. She didn't look as starchy as Miss Crewell, and she wasn't as mean as her, either. Mrs. Davies was cute and tiny. She could sure yell though. We all jumped when she raised her voice. She had children, as did some of the other matrons, and seemed to understand our longing to be home. Mrs. Reed, on the other hand, was just plain old mean. According to her, we could never do anything right. She liked to give the strap a lot, even if we hadn't done anything really bad. She was forever scolding someone.

Not all the matrons were mean to us though. Mrs. Armstrong was on staff for quite a while, and she was always kind. She had soft curly hair and smelled nice. I never heard her yell or scream, nor did I ever see her strap anyone. When she wanted something done she'd ask me nicely, and I'd willingly do the task. She had a way about her that made me want to please her. I think most of the children liked Mrs. Armstrong. Maybe the reason she was so nice was that she had several children of her own. They went to school with us, and were friendly. They lived just across the street from the school. Just by looking at them I could tell they weren't rich, but they were happy. It kind of reminded me of my family.

I always felt Mrs. Armstrong understood our plight, and tried hard to make us feel we weren't abandoned. Sometimes I even wanted to call her Auntie for real, but I knew I mustn't. Not only would I be in trouble with the other children, but Mrs. Armstrong might get in trouble with the other matrons if they ever found out how nice she was to us when none of them was around.

* * *

On the way to school we had to cross over a bridge. When the water was in full spate it could be pretty scary, but during the summer we could walk from one side of the river to the other, jumping from stone to stone, without getting our feet wet. Once during low water Alex carved 'HC + AB' in a heart into one of the pilings.

"Preserved forever," he said with satisfaction as he folded his penknife and put it back in his pocket.

"What did you do that for?" I asked.

"Because I want everyone to know I love you!"

Alex could be quite a charmer, so I was never entirely sure whether to trust him or not. One day in school I was allowed to leave early because I'd done well on a test. I was also able to choose a friend to leave early with me. I chose a girlfriend to come with me, and Alex never forgave me. He said he'd held his breath as I was making my decision, and was heartbroken when I chose someone else. He was fun to be around, so we remained good, close friends throughout our years in New Denver, but never did become boyfriend and girlfriend.

Just before the end of term we had our school photos done. Mine looked just like my friend, Suzy Hashimoto's. We were both wearing the same bad dresses, and our haircuts were exactly the same; longer on one side than the other, and kind of ratty on the ends. We looked like twins, except that her hair was darker. And, of course, that she had Japanese features whereas mine were European.

I'd loved my braids, when I had them. I'd always felt so pretty when they'd just been done and I didn't have my hair in my eyes. Now it always looked terrible. I couldn't wait to grow up so I could go to a hairdresser whenever I wanted. Maybe I'd even be a hairdresser; then I could always do my hair in exactly the style I liked.

We were always thinking how much better things would be when we were no longer children. We all knew the main advantage of being grown up was that then no one could boss you around, or tell you how and when to do things. We'd even heard you could be lazy if you wanted to, and they couldn't stop you.

10. LEARNING TO SWIM

Summer, 1956

Even if we didn't get to go home, at least summer meant no school, which meant there'd be time for sports and swimming and lazing by the lake.

"But haven't you heard? Old Jackass has organized work periods during the summer break."

"So what? Just cause school's out doesn't mean the floors won't need sweeping, same as always."

"No, I mean on top of the regular chores! We do them in the morning. Then in the afternoons he wants us to weed the beach and stuff!"

"What?"

"No way!"

"If it's that important to him, he can weed it himself!"

The next thing I heard was that a swimming instructor had been hired for the summer, to keep us busy when we weren't doing the extra chores Stickler had laid on. I'd never learned to swim; the only water sport I knew was running through the sprinkler. The idea of swimming in the huge lake frightened and excited me at the same time.

The day the swimming instructor arrived we all gathered one hour after lunch. When he'd introduced himself and given us the swimming rules, he split us up into classes according to our abilities. I was in the beginners swim class; one of many who'd never swum a stroke in her life. Some of the other children were in intermediate, and a few of the older ones in senior. I was impressed. Imagine swimming like a senior!

Since I couldn't swim, a couple of my girlfriends offered to help me learn before the lesson.

"It's always easier when you already know how."

"And it'll make the instructor happy."

"But..."

"Don't worry."

"It's normal to be anxious."

"But..."

"You'll be fine."

"And besides, what can possibly go wrong?"

Despite my doubts, the girls took me by the hand and led me gently into the lake. As we went further from shore the water came up to my knees, my waist, my neck. I was on tippy-toes, trying not to swallow mouthfuls of lake water, when the bottom suddenly fell away and I found my feet flailing, with nothing underneath them for support.

"Don't worry!"

"We've got you!"

My surge of panic melted away as I realized my two friends had me securely by the arms and were calmly treading water. Their composure gave me confidence. My head was still above water. I wasn't going to sink.

"Now kick your legs."

"Back and forth... slowly... that's right."

"You've got it!"

"Feels good, doesn't it?"

I nodded. In truth, I was so tense I could barely wiggle my toes, but I didn't want to disappoint them.

Then the unthinkable happened.

They let go.

I floundered. I threw my arms up, and down I went. Down, down, down. I sank to the bottom like a rock. It seemed I was down there forever, but up I came, gagging and sputtering and choking, and crying my eyes out. I was furious, and my friends were laughing their heads off.

"I don't believe it! This is just like that skating lesson!"

"Don't just thrash about; swim!"

"I can't believe anyone any more!"

"Kick! Kick your feet, and swim!"

Blind rage took over. I started to kick like crazy. "I hate you! I hate you! I hate you!" My legs were sore from kicking, and my arms felt like they were going to fall off, but at least I wasn't drowning. Then the realization hit me.

I wasn't drowning.

"Hey, I'm swimming!" I was almost hysterical. "I can't believe it! I'm swimming! I'm actually swimming!" I shouted and waved, and thrashed until I could touch bottom. Anger and elation and relief and ingratitude surged within me.

"Oh, and thanks for the lesson! Murderers!"

I was disappointed no one stopped them from almost drowning me. The matrons and the instructor weren't aware of anything that was going on. I went back in the water, and the girls kept an eye on me while I swam in the shallows. One easy lesson and I was on my way.

* * *

Any time we didn't put our dirty laundry in the outgoing container we had to quickly do it ourselves before a snooping matron came on it and punished us. I'd already found myself in that situation a couple of times, and it wasn't pleasant, so Ruby and I decided we needed to find something to help make it easier.

It was a fine sunny day, and we were exploring the Japanese village just beyond the dorm. This was a neighbourhood of small houses, most of which had well-kept yards with grass neatly trimmed and flowers in bloom all summer long. As we strolled through the lanes behind the houses we checked in the garbage cans left out for pickup. We'd found treasures that way before, and now rarely went past a bin without taking a peek inside.

That day we scored big time. There on top of a garbage can lay an old-fashioned washboard. We could hardly believe our luck. We brushed the cobwebs off, screeching as the spiders scurried away. The glass had a huge crack in it, but the wood was solid. We hurried back to the dorm, skipping on air, overjoyed at the convenience it represented. We'd just have to rub our laundry on the ridges and it'd be clean. No more rubbing hand against hand.

"Do you think we'll get in trouble?"

"What for?"

"This."

"Why should we?"

"Someone might think we stole it."

"Who?"

"I don't know... the Hisser... any of them."

"You figure we should hide it?"

"From her, at least."

We smuggled it past the guardhouse, and into the pink room. There we scrubbed it clean, then stood back to admire our prize. We agreed it was too dangerous to store in our lockers, so we planned to hide it outside on the property as soon as we could. Before we did though, we showed it off to whoever was interested, proud of our little find.

Ruby and I had promised earlier not to fight over anything we found, and we didn't. Once when we'd discovered a piece of jewelry and each wanted it, we just took turns wearing it. So this time we marked the washboard with both our numbers, and loaned it out to anyone who needed it. There were plenty of takers, because there was always someone with dirty laundry that needed doing by hand. At one point we actually thought about renting it out and making some money, but quickly changed our minds when we thought about how much bigger and tougher some of the girls were who borrowed it, and how easy it would be for them simply to gang up on us and take it away. This way at least it was ours, and a certain amount of respect was bestowed on us for sharing our good fortune.

Usually Auntie Vatkin drove my parents to New Denver for visiting day. My auntie was hesitant to go long distances by herself, but I guess with my parents in the car her fears were lessened. She'd usually be in charge of my sisters when they came, and would be kept fairly busy. But she often brought gifts for me, and always smothered me with hugs and kisses.

One visiting day my auntie brought me a doll. It was a boy doll, the same size as a real baby, but he looked as if he was two years old. He was dressed in blue corduroy pants and jacket, with a plaid collar and cuffs. He also had a jaunty hat perched on his head that matched his outfit. He was the most beautiful doll I'd ever seen. Even the Eaton's catalogue didn't have a doll like him. There was no special reason for the gift - my auntie just brought it for me. It was a wonderful surprise, and I was so happy I cried.

I named the doll Jimmy, and he quickly became my best friend. I liked to pretend he was a real person. I hugged and kissed him all the time, and told him I was so sorry he had to live in New Denver with me, that he'd be much happier living in Grand Forks with my little sisters. I often took him on walks with me, and sometimes we just sat on the beach. Other than that he stayed on my bed.

Jimmy liked to visit with the other girls, and the other girls all wanted to hold him too, so I let them. I'd let him sleep over sometimes when a girl was sick, especially if she wouldn't be going to school. But he always liked me best. I loved him so much and took really good care of him. He always knew I'd hug and kiss my children when I grew up.

Jimmy became a huge part of my stay in New Denver. I liked that I could tell him all my hopes and fears and he understood, and that I could share my most secret thoughts and feelings with him and he never told anyone else. At night I'd cuddle him, and sleep easier because he was there with me. He made life in New Denver much easier to bear.

11. KISSING THROUGH CHAIN LINK

Summer, 1956

I generally enjoyed each visit that first summer in New Denver. After so long away from Mama, it felt like heaven to have her arms around me, holding me tight. We'd find a shady spot under a tree overlooking the lake. Dad spread a blanket on the ground, and my mother would lay out the food while Auntie Vatkin kept an eye on my sisters. The food was always good. My mother would serve up her best borscht, followed by wonderfully gooey chocolate cake, or home-made doughnuts. Sitting on the blanket, my little sisters huddled so close to me that sometimes we were like one person instead of three. I'd tell them what I'd been up to, while I hugged and kissed them. They'd share their stories with me, all the while love shining in their dancing eyes. It was a dream in which all that mattered was that I was on a picnic in the sunshine with my beloved family, sharing wonderful stories with my sisters, and giggling like the silly little children that we were.

Those moments never lasted, though. Sooner or later the harsh reality of where I was would hit, and in the middle of a laugh I'd suddenly cling to my sisters, bury my face in their hair, and pour out my pain and longing in a series of desperate, choking, heartfelt sobs. I wanted to tell them how it was there. No adult really cared about us. There was no one there to kiss a hurt away, or to give a hug when we needed one. When any one of us got sick we'd have our temperature taken; if it wasn't too bad, we'd be told 'school as usual'; if it was worse, we'd be left in bed. When it was serious the child was put in the pink room, or got sent to the hospital.

Stop thinking like that, I told myself. *They're not here long. Pay attention for the short time you have with your family.*

Then, before I knew it, it was time to say goodbye. My parents' arms felt so warm around me as they hugged me and whispered in my ear. They'd always remind me to be a good girl, to behave myself, and work hard in school. One more hug and kiss, and away they'd go.

Life in New Denver was hard, but I was getting used to it and learning to survive. My family's hugs and kisses were what gave me the strength to endure the next two weeks until it was time to see them all again. And bad as things were, I could at least console myself with the thought that they couldn't possibly get any worse.

* * *

One day that summer we came on some older boys from the dorm digging holes in the dry-baked earth around the perimeter of the dormitory grounds.

"What are you doing that for?"

"Don't know. They just told us to."

Tall posts were set in the holes. When the concrete footings had hardened, rolls of chain-link fencing arrived and the boys helped put that up too. They felt bad about doing it, but they'd been threatened with punishment if they didn't, so they did as they were told. Some of the older boys were pretty darn big, but they were no match for some of the male caregivers. On occasion we'd see a boy or two covered with bruises, or with darkness around the eyes, and of course we'd question them. They never told exactly what had happened, just that there'd been trouble.

It was a surreal experience, like watching the inmates of a jail walling themselves in. When they were finished, an eight-foot-high steel chain-link security fence surrounded the dorm. It formed a U-shape, from one end down by the lake, up and around the large dormitory, the annex, the laundry and the gymnasium, and back down to the lake. The property was completely enclosed on three sides, the lake being the fourth side. I'd only seen fences like that in magazines, when they showed pictures of prisons. There was a big main gate at the entrance so vehicles could drive through, and a smaller pedestrian gate for people to walk through. The main gate was hardly ever opened, but the small one was almost never shut. We were still free to come and go. So why the fence?

In a sense, nothing had changed. We were still the same captives in the same unlocked jail; a jail we were free to leave, but to which we had to return. But with the coming of the fence a new isolation descended on us. We were still alone, still far from home; but now we were cooped up like a bunch of chickens in a cage. Life became different then. We'd file through the pedestrian gate one by one or, in the case of really thin children, two by two. Whenever we asked a member of staff whose idea the fence was, the most we ever got was 'someone in authority.' When we asked why it had been put up, we were never told. Whatever the reason, the rest of New Denver, where people lived with their families in houses they called home, may as well have been in a different universe.

But still, why the fence? As I lay awake turning it over in my mind, a new possibility hit me. Maybe the fence wasn't there to keep us in.

Maybe the fence was there to keep people out.

* * *

The first visiting day after the fence went up was awful. Our parents approached the gate, spoke to the authorities, and then stayed outside. Parents and children spread out along the perimeter, and visited standing on different sides of the fence while armed police patrolled with dogs. Under-aged children were allowed inside. But when my sisters tried to carry my mother's borscht and pyrahi throught the gate, the guards said any food parcels now had to be sent to the kitchens, and we'd get them later. So Kathrine returned the food to my father, who scraped a channel and passed it under the fence to me. She and Marie came inside to be with me, while I ate and ate and ate until I could hardly breathe.

Although my sisters were too young to be taken from home and kept with me in residence, it frightened them to hear the clang of the gate as it swung shut behind them. I hugged them and assured them they wouldn't have to stay, and tried not to let my terror for them show. But as long as they were on the inside their eyes darted back and forth, always watching. They held to the fence as though it gave them some kind of security. So I hugged my sisters, and resolved only to cry when visiting day was over.

"But why won't they let you inside?" I asked my parents.

The answer was complicated, and involved the signing of papers and matters of principle.

"What! You chose to stay outside? But how could you?"

"It's not that simple, Helen."

"You'll understand when you're older."

That visit was a blur. When it came time to say goodbye I couldn't even remember what we'd said. We went back to our beds and stood to attention. The matrons did their usual head count to make sure no one had sneaked away unnoticed. I wondered how they thought that could be possible, with guards on the gate and no room under the fence. Dad could hardly pass the food under, they'd made it so tight.

I'd read somewhere that if you grow up without human contact you become like a wild animal. I wondered whether any of the other children thought the same thing, and if so, what kind of animal they'd be. I'd be a panther. Then I'd be able to run fast, and scare everyone. On second thoughts though, I couldn't be a panther because they eat meat.

When the dormitory was first established, visiting time had been in the mornings. As children were brought in from farther and farther afield, the previous director had moved it to the afternoons, to make visiting easier for parents with a long way to travel. A month or so after the fence went up visiting time was moved back to the mornings. My parents now had to travel up from Grand Forks on the Saturday, staying overnight at friends' houses in the Kootenays, so they could get to New Denver on time for the new ten o'clock Sunday morning visiting hour.

I wondered often in those early months why I'd been sent to New Denver when my mother had been teaching me perfectly well at home. Then one day I overheard an older girl say, "They don't want to educate us. They want to assimilate us."

I'd never heard the word 'assimilate' before, and wondered what it meant.

When I got to school the next day I asked the teacher, but she seemed a little guarded in her reply. So I looked it up. I was used to looking up long words in the dictionary from listening to my father. I learned that it meant to eradicate all minority traits so that everyone behaves in conformity with the majority. I had to look up 'eradicate' too, and I might have had to look up 'conformity', just to check that it meant what I thought it meant.

I was stunned. Was that really what the government intended for us?

But why, when we were already Canadian?

What could they do to make us more Canadian?

I'd never been tempted by the long skirts, headscarves and aprons of my maternal grandmother. I was Canadian right down to the jeans and runners that were part of my everyday dress. I liked borscht, but I liked french fries too. Then it hit me. That was why we were forbidden to speak Russian in the dorm. It was a trait that made us different, and so they wanted to eradicate it. I'd assumed our caregivers were doing it just to be mean, as a way of imposing their absolute control over us. It never occurred to me it was a deliberate policy of the government, decided in council meetings by the people's elected representatives.

But what's so important about a language, I wondered. Lots of people spoke other languages and it didn't prevent them from being Canadian. Why was it so important we forget our mother tongue? They might as well ask us to forget our own name. Again it hit me. That wasn't hard to do at all. After all, I was now number eighty-five.

With a burst of amazement I suddenly understood why, when the time came to sing 'God Save The Queen' or 'O Canada!' in school, the Freedomite children always remained silent. I loved to sing, but I knew if anyone, especially from the dorm, were to see me singing either national anthem I'd be in big trouble. And if word ever got back to my parents and my grandparents they'd be really mad at me, too. I'd always assumed the reason was that we were Russian as well, and that therefore it would be a contradiction to sing it. After all, we never got together to sing the Russian national anthem, either. I realized now it was a defiant stand, not against the country but against a government that had welcomed us in and promised us protection, and who were now actively trying to destroy our culture.

Well, I didn't want to become just like anyone else. I liked who I was. And if the government thought our way of life was important enough to destroy, that to my mind made it important enough to be worth preserving. That very same day I wrote home telling my family I wanted to start learning to read and write Russian.

When he next came up, my father brought with him two Russian textbooks. They were beginner's books, very basic. I wrote my name and the number eighty-five inside, and straight away he began teaching me my first lesson, through the fence. The first thing I had to do was learn the letters, so he sounded each of them out and I wrote down the pronunciation in English beside them. I was determined to claim my heritage, so I could make my parents and grandparents proud and so I'd be able to pass on my heritage to my children in turn. Besides, I figured it would be neat to be able to read and write using two different alphabets. And I wanted to be able to write letters in Russian to my auntie, because I knew she couldn't read English well. After my parents left I practiced on my own for hours, and every two weeks I proudly showed my father what I'd learned.

I also practiced Russian hymns from another book, so I could sing along better on visiting days. The book was beautiful, and I wanted to keep it forever so I could show it to my children when I was grown up. I was worried Matron would take it away from me, but I was allowed to keep it. I always loved singing, no matter what language it was in, and a few of us would sometimes practice together. It was hard work though, because even though my parents and my grandparents all sang, I found it hard to carry a tune.

My younger sisters told me they too were learning to read and write in Russian. They'd begun attending a Russian school in Gilpin, about seven miles from our home in Grand Forks. Mr. Patko, the teacher, would pick them up at our home, and then drive to Gilpin. To get to the school they had to cross a river by means of a swinging footbridge. Some of the boys would usually be waiting on the other side, and would swing the bridge madly until Mr. Patko yelled at them to stop. They then walked down a dusty dirt road to the one-room schoolhouse. The lessons were fun. They learned a lot, improved their writing skills, and enjoyed each other's company.

But the fear of discovery was always with them, as they never knew when the police would raid the school. The floor was full of knotholes, and Kathrine would tell of watching the police walking slowly among the younger children above them while she and the older children hid below and tried not to be heard. After what seemed like hours the coast would be clear, and they'd come out from under the building and race for the outhouse, desperate to be first in the door. The whole story would be relayed to me with breathless excitement the next visiting day. As I listened I could see the pain my mom was going through. With one child in New Denver, and two at home in hiding, life must have been hell for her and Dad, as well as for all the other parents.

That September brought my ninth birthday, the first I'd celebrated away from home. In the ten months since I'd arrived in New Denver I'd learned how to lie. That was very hard for me, because I'd never, ever lied to my parents. I'd learned how to steal too. Sometimes there'd be candy on Matron's desk, and I'd be so hungry I'd take some when she wasn't looking. I never stole from Taro though, because he was always so kind to us. I'd also learned all kinds of new words. Sometimes I even made myself blush when I used them. If my mom could have heard me swear I'm sure she'd have prayed extra hard for me. When I lived at home I'd never needed to lie or swear or steal. In New Denver I quickly learned all of these traits. My friends and I stuck up for each other, lied for each other, and protected each other as best we could. We had to, in order to survive.

But I'd also come to learn that I couldn't necessarily trust these same friends, however loyal they might seem to be. Even though they were close enough to share secrets with, I still had to remember not to let my true emotions show. If the other children really understood me, no matter how good friends they were, there was always the possibility they might turn on me. I couldn't forget the times I was taught to skate, or to swim, or how to use the floor polisher.

So I reminded myself always to hold back. Only when no one knew what was going on in my mind could I hope to be safe. I couldn't ever show any weakness, or the other children would make my life a living hell. It was hard to pretend I was tough when I felt so scared I could pee myself.

I just wanted to be a normal kid, but I didn't feel much like a kid any more. Sometimes I didn't even like myself. I still hoped that maybe when I got older I might be a good person, but right now, I figured, it didn't pay to be good.

I'm sure my parents noticed the difference in me, but it was my Auntie Annie who first put it into words.

"Why, whatever's the matter with you, Helen?" she gasped, on first catching sight of me one visiting day.

"Nothing," I said, in the flat voice I now slipped into so easily when I was determined not to give anything away.

"But when you lived at home you always had such beautiful, smiling eyes!"

I hastily broadened my face into what I believed was an expression of radiant good cheer.

My aunt was not taken in. "You're smiling," she told me, "but your eyes..." Auntie Annie shook her head sadly. "Helen... your eyes are dead!"

* * *

Tad Mori, the guard, was always willing to join in any activity we came up with. One time he and Taro tried to teach us Japanese. I enjoyed the challenge of learning a totally new language. It was hard, but we had a lot of fun trying to sound like them when we spoke. Soon we could count to ten, and say 'Thank you.' They even taught us little rhymes we could all sing together. Taro was pleased when we thanked him in his mother tongue for things we bought in his store. Some of us tried to teach them a few words of Russian, but we weren't successful.

We also learned to use our own sign language among ourselves, and unless you were in the little circle you wouldn't have any idea what was going on. The boys had a language of their own as well, something along the lines of pig latin, which they perfected to the nth degree. We were their friends, and we had no idea what was being said. We even had a system in place so we could deliver messages to the boys after lights out. A combination of coughs and knocks on the wall between the annex bedrooms, and the message would be received. Matron couldn't hear from the office, and we'd often continue for a long time until someone yelled at us to shut up. Then Matron would come bustling in, and we'd all pretend to be asleep.

Tad lived in the village, and his home was close to the dorm. It was so neat and clean we thought his wife did all the work, but to the best of my remembrance, Tad was single. He took the time to talk to us. He asked about our home life and our families. It was nice to know he cared. He also used to tell us stories about Vancouver, which was where he used to live.

"It sounds as if you liked it there."

"I did!"

"Then why did you move to New Denver?"

"I didn't choose to. The government made a lot of Japanese people move up here during the war. Where we live now was used as an internment camp. This school dormitory was a sanatorium for those of us who got tuberculosis."

"Where are they all now?"

"After the war the government sent most of them away. If they didn't go to other parts of Canada they were sent to Japan."

"Even if they'd been born in Canada?" I asked.

"Yes, even then."

"What if they couldn't speak Japanese?"

"They still had to go."

I was silent for a moment.

"Why didn't you go?"

"Anyone who was sick or old and had no one to care for them was allowed to stay on."

"Why did the government move you here?"

"I guess they thought we might be spies."

I had believed it was because of his empathy for the suffering of little children that Tad understood what it was like for us to be forcibly removed from our homes. It never occurred to me that he'd been through a similar upheaval himself. And then it hit me that that was why my friend Suzy was in New Denver. In fact, everyone in the Japanese village was there for the same reason - because they were suspected of being spies. In that instant, any lingering self-pity I may have felt evaporated, to be replaced by a deep and lasting compassion for anyone treated unfairly, whatever their circumstances.

Photo Gallery

Above - The Annex of the New Denver Sanatorium, later renamed the New Denver School Dormitory. The younger children were housed here.

Right - In Grade One, with my bad haircut and dormitory-issue clothes.

Helen Chernoff Freeman

Above - My parents visit, Christmas 1955. I had been in New Denver less than a month when this photo was taken.

Above right - Visiting day at New Denver, before the fence went up. I am wearing the blue jacket with white piping my aunt had given me one Christmas.

Below right - With my father on visiting day. "My father, John Chernoff, was a real giant of a man. He was handsome, with broad, powerful shoulders and the most beautiful blue eyes." He was working as a logger at the time this photo was taken.

Left - With 'trailblazer' Auntie Annie Vatkin (left) and my mother. "[My grandparents] had six children. Only my mother, Mary, the youngest, and my aunt Annie, the oldest, survived to adulthood."

Above - With my maternal grandmother Anastasia Zebroff. Visiting was always outdoors, however harsh the weather

Left - With then-youngest sister Marie during my first year in New Denver. "I loved to hold her and cuddle her, because in my world she was my doll number two."

Above - In the cowboy hat I liked to wear when re-enacting scenes from movies we watched on Saturday nights.

Left - Girls number eighty-five (left) and fifty-eight, in dormitory-issue jackets and jeans.

Above - Me (far right) and friends with Tad Mori, one of the guards at the New Denver School Dormitory. Tadi, as he was affectionately known by the children, had himself been removed to New Denver by the government, along with other Canadians of Japanese descent, during the Second World War.

Above - Swimming in Slocan Lake with friends. Behind are the raft we liked to dive from and the rope marking off the area permitted for swimming. Beyond, telephone wires indicate the road to the Cape, taken by parents on visiting days.

Below - An eight-foot high chain-link fence was put up in August, 1956. Thereafter, visits took place with parents on one side of the fence and children on the other.

Above - I am behind the fence, my mother and sisters Kathrine (right) and Marie (left) are in front. "I longed for the touch of my family during visits, but the holes in the fence were only big enough to allow my fingers through."

Below - Youngest sister Marie joins me behind the fence; next-eldest sister Kathrine remains outside. "Although my sisters were too young to be taken from home and kept with me in residence, it frightened them to hear the clang of the gate as it swung shut behind them."

Above left - My maternal grandfather John Zebroff joins my mother and sister Kathrine on visiting day. "Grandpa Zebroff was tall, very dark-skinned from a lifetime of working in the open air, and had a full beard and moustache." He was the son of Nicholas Zebroff, who founded the Sons of Freedom not long after the Doukhobors' arrival in Canada.

Below left - A sad farewell. "Even before the visit was over my heart would be breaking, knowing they'd be going home and leaving me behind."

Above - 'Jimmy', given to me by my Auntie Annie, helped comfort me – and some of my friends – during my time in New Denver.

Above - In Grade Two, wearing a beautiful sweater with rhinestones on.

Above right - With my maternal grandparents, John and Anastasia Zebroff. "[Grandpa] refused to speak to us in English, first of all because Grandma wouldn't understand, and secondly ...so we didn't forget our language, our heritage and our culture."

Below right - In all, I spent three years and eight months in the New Denver School Dormitory. During most of that time I was unable to touch my parents except through the chain-link fence which surrounded the grounds.

Above - Visiting day in winter. Families would hang blankets over the fence to try and shelter their children from the worst of the weather.

Below - With my parents. A food parcel brought by them is at my feet. Not long after this photo was taken all gifts of food had to be handed over to staff, often never to be seen again.

Above right - Eating borscht from a flask brought by my mother. One of the joys of visiting day was tasting my mother's delicious food.

Below right - Even a thermos of home-cooked borscht could not take away the pain of not being able to feel my mother's loving arms around me.

Above - Families pray at the main gate on visiting day.

Right - With my family, May 1958. For one day only, children from the dormitory were allowed into town with their families to take part in New Denver's centenary celebrations. "We had such a beautiful visit."

Helen Chernoff Freeman

Left - In Grade Three, wearing the scarf and brooch my father bought me in Paris.

Above - Wearing a dress my mother made. (The name 'Helen' can just be seen embroidered on the pocket.) The guard hut is in the background.

GROUSE MOUNTAIN CHAIR LIFT
VANCOUVER. CANADA · 1958

Above - My terrifying ride with the Dormitory director's wife in a chairlift on Grouse Mountain, North Vancouver.

Right - Singing and dancing with friends on the verandah.

Above - Officers of the Royal Canadian Mounted Police (here seen over my left shoulder) were present at every visit.

Right - In Grade Four, wearing the necklace I won in a spelling bee.

Above left - Children from diverse backgrounds attended the New Denver elementary school. In this Fourth Grade class photo I am standing in the centre of the back row.

Below left - All children were released on August 2nd, 1959 after our parents had agreed to send us to public school. Here children wait to board the buses which took us to Krestova, where we were reunited with our parents.

Above - My first day home after leaving New Denver, August 1959. Left to right: sister Marie, grandfather John Zebroff, me, auntie Anne Vatkin, grandmother Anastasia Zebroff, sister Kathrine.

ROYAL CANADIAN MOUNTED POLICE A-40

RADIOGRAM

Message No.	Time Sent:	Time Received:	Date:

RR 2 2320 Z   2-12-55.

FM: NELSON SUB/DIVISION
TO: C.I.B.

NR

16/2

SEARCHES THIS DATE GRAND FORKS AREA HAS RESULTED IN APPREHENSION
ONE DOUKHOBOR CHILD NOT ATTENDING SCHOOL. JUVENILE COURT
HAS COMMITTED CHILD TO INSTITUTION AT NEW DENVER. FURTHER
SEARCHES BEING CARRIED OUT.

N.C.O. i/c, R.C.M.P., GRAND FORKS, B.C.

1. Copy. Please expedite report on the
apprehension of this child.

S/D.D.D. - RETURN MAIL

Helen CHERNOFF - age 8.

(▇▇▇▇▇▇) Insp.,
Commanding Nelson Sub-Division.
Nelson, B.C. 12-1-56.

Above - The report recording my apprehension by police on 2nd December, 1955.

*Right - The police report of my committal by a magistrate to the care and custody of the
Superintendent of Child Welfare under the Protection of Children Act, 3rd January, 1956.*

FORM C264P
1901-[1·51 (142)   P.C.R. **First Report**   H. Q. FILE NO.   DIV. FILE NO.

ROYAL CANADIAN MOUNTED POLICE

DATE 12-January-1956.

B.DIVISION Nelson.   S. DIV. REF.

DETACHMENT Grand Forks(Org. Terr.)   DET. REF. 55-3-20.   A.R.V. NO. N/A.

DEFENDANT (A) Helen CHERNOFF (Juv. 8 yrs.)   ADDRESS Grand Forks, B.C.

OCCUPATION Student.   STATUS IN CANADA (B) Canadian Born.

NATIONALITY Canadian   RACE Russian.   DATE OF BIRTH Not known.

PLACE & DATE OF OFFENCE Grand Forks, B.C. 2/12-55.

OFFENCE (C) Protection of Children's Act. Sec. 7 (m).

INFORMATION (D) Sgt. ▓▓▓▓▓, 2/12-55, ▓▓▓▓▓▓, S/M., Grand Forks, B.C.

DATE OF ARREST OR SUMMONS APPREHENDED: 2/12-55.   PLACE & DATE OF TRIAL Grand Forks, B.C. 3/1-56.

MAGISTRATE OR JUDGE (E) Stipendiary Magistrate   METHOD OF TRIAL (F) Summary Conv.   PLEA None taken.

PROSECUTOR OR PROS'G COUNSEL Sgt. ▓▓▓▓▓, R.C.M.Police.   DEFENCE COUNSEL Nil.

DISPOSITION OF CHARGE OR SENTENCE IMPOSED AND DATE ORDER MADE: Committed to the care and custody of the Superintendent of Child Welfare. 3/1-56.

FINE PAID OR GAOL TERM TAKEN Taken to school at New Denver,B.C. by the local Welfare representative, Mr. ▓▓▓▓▓.

COSTS POLICE: IMPOSED   COLLECTED   AUTHORITY FOR SEARCH N/A.

	IMPOSED	COLLECTED	
SERVING SUMMONS	$		COMPLAINANT Sgt. ▓▓▓▓▓, R.C.M.P.
ARREST	$		
ATTENDING COURT	$		
WITNESS FEES (POLICE)	$		FINGERPRINTS TO H. Q. N/a. (DATE)
MILEAGE MILES @	$		
TOTAL	$ Nil	Nil	PHOTOGRAPH TO H. Q. N/A. (DATE)

COSTS OTHER THAN POLICE   LAST PREVIOUS CONVICTION (QUOTE F. P. S. NUMBER, IF KNOWN)

MAGISTRATE'S FEES	$	Not known here.
WITNESSES	$	
TOTAL COSTS	$ Nil	Nil

WITNESSES:-   PROSECUTION Sgt. ▓▓▓▓▓, RCMP.   DEFENCE Nil.

REMARKS (G) 1.   The above case arose and was delt with as shown above when information was received that the subject was residing at the home of her parents Mr. & Mrs. John CHERNOFF of Grand Forks, B.C., was the age of 8 years and was not attending school. As the parents a are Doukhobors and of the "Sons-of-Freedom" sect it was not their in- tention to ever send the child to school.
2.   Committal forms have been duly completed, original being forwarded to the Supt. of Child Welfare, Victoria,B.C. and a copy to the local Social Worker, Mr. ▓▓▓▓▓.

DIARY DATE CONCLUDED HERE.   INVESTIGATED BY   Sgd.   Cst. (▓▓▓▓▓)# Grand Forks Detachment.

FW'D ON 13/1 56,   TO O.C.S./-DIV. FW'D ON   1956   TO O.C. DIV.   FW'D COMMISSIONER (DATE)   (DATE)   (DATE)

Sgd.   Sgt.   Sgd.   Insp.   Sgd.   Supt.
(▓▓▓▓▓ I/C DETACHMENT,)-SEE REVERSE SIDE OF   I/C SUB DIVISION   )E), (F.) A I/C., DIVISION C.I.B.

RCMP—5680

ROYAL CANADIAN MO TED POLICE

C. 237

DIVISION FILE NO.

DIVISION
"E"

SUB-DIVISION
Nelson

DETACHMENT
Grand Forks

PROVINCE British Columbia   DATE August 7th, 1959

RE: Helen Chernoff (Juv. 8 yrs.)(B.D.   ) Grand Forks, B.C.
Protection of Children's Act (7'm) - Grand Forks, B.C.
(GRAND FORKS DETM. CASE)(ORG) (ASST. TO SOCIAL WELFARE)

HEADQUARTERS

1.   With reference to the above, previous correspondence submitted in this regard dated 12-1-56, please be advised of the following.

SUB-DIVISION

2.   As a result of an application submitted by Mary J. and John M. CHERNOFF, Grand Forks, B.C. to ████████, S/M, Nelson, B.C. for the release of the above child from the Dormitory School, New Denver, B.C. a hearing was had on July 30th, 1959 at 1:00 PM, before ████████, S/M in the Court House at Grand Forks, B.C.

DETACHMENT
55-3-20

3.   At the above mentioned hearing ████████, Barrister appeared for the Crown. Both parents took the stand individually, were sworn over the traditional Doukhobour bread, salt and water. Each parent made a promise that if their child was released from New Denver that they would enroll them in a Public School in September, 1959 in their School District. Mag. ████ reserved his decision on this case till Friday, July 31st, 1959 at 11AM in Nelson, B.C.

P.C.R.
12-1-56 G.F.

4.   On the latter date Mag. ████ gave his decision that the above child was to be released from New Denver to the parents and to be enrolled in a Public School in September of 1959.

A.R.V. No.

5.   Other participants at this hearing were, ████████, School Attendance Officer, Nelson, B.C. and ████████, Interpreter. Extra copies attached.

"CONCLUDED HERE"

(Sgd. ████)#████   Cpl.
N.C.O. i/c Detm.

(Sgd. ████)#████   Cst.
Grand Forks Detm.

O.C. "E" DIVISION
R.C.M.P. VICTORIA
For your information.

DIARY DATE

SET FOR   Nil

Insp.
Commanding Nelson S/Division

FILE NUMBERS, HEADING AND MARGINAL REFERENCE ARE TO BE PROPERLY FILLED IN

The police record of the magistrate's decision given on 31st July, 1959, to release me from the New Denver School Dormitory.

12. DISSATISFACTION

Fall, 1956

One night the slop they served for dinner was worse than anything they'd tried to make us eat before. It was a kind of stew, and smelled awful. Closer inspection revealed gray, unidentifiable lumps, bits of orange rind, and a clump of floating hair.

"I'm not eating this crap," one of the girls said, pushing her plate away.

Some of the girls tried to eat it, but they were gagging. I didn't even try to put any of it in my mouth. I took the toilet paper and plastic bag out of my pocket and slipped the so-called food into it and then into my pocket. I smeared some of the remains on my face, dirtied my cutlery, moved the plate around, and then buttered some bread and ate that.

Suddenly I became aware that the table had fallen silent. I heard Miss Crewell breathing behind me.

"What's going on here?" she demanded.

No one answered. Girls looked down, or prodded their food with their spoons.

"Well?"

One girl spoke up. "Er... the food's not very good tonight, Miss Crewell."

"Not very good?" Matron noticed my empty plate. "I see Helen's managed to eat it all. How was it, Helen?"

"Umm... okay. I guess."

"Would you like a second helping?"

"No, thank you."

By now the whole room was silent. Miss Crewell surveyed the numerous plates of uneaten stew in the dining hall.

"You will all eat your dinners," she announced.

"But, Miss Crewell..."

"Anyone who doesn't eat will be punished!"

At this threat some of the children reluctantly resumed eating the foul slurry in front of them. When the clink of spoons on plates had died down, Matron went through the room identifying those who hadn't eaten.

"You will return to your bedrooms now. The rest of you can go out and play; or you can go to bed along with those being punished."

We scattered like marbles. None of us wanted to go to bed that early.

Once outside we went round to the back of the annex to see just what kind of punishment the girls were going to get. The annex windows were not too high, so we scrambled up the wall like monkeys and looked through the window. Miss Crewell had them lie stiff on their beds, fully dressed, with their arms by their sides. They looked just like soldiers, only they were lying down.

"You will remain there until morning," she said. "Anyone who moves an inch will be severely punished."

"Please, Miss Crewell, may I go to the bathroom?"

"You will neither talk nor move until I say!"

"But Miss Crewell..."

"Silence!"

When Matron left the room we tapped on the window and made faces at the girls lying there unable to move. We were often cruel to one another, and this was one of those times. "You got caught and we didn't!" we taunted, and then ran for cover when Matron reappeared in the doorway. *I should be in the army when I grow up*, I thought. *I'd probably have made a good captain.* I already knew how to follow rules and regulations, and I could easily think up all sorts of mean punishments.

Those children went hungry. There were no cookies for snacks, no glasses of warm milk. In the middle of the night I was awakened by the sobs of one of the girls who hadn't eaten. She had tummy ache from the hunger.

"Shut up and go to sleep," Matron yelled. "And next time you'll eat what's placed in front of you!"

The sobs continued.

"And if this nonsense doesn't stop, you'll get the strap!"

* * *

The more time I spent in New Denver, the more I realized that some adults take a great deal of pleasure in being bullies. We weren't allowed to use the word hate at home, but in New Denver I used it all the time. I hated the matrons, the principal, some of the guards, and the bigger bully kids.

My mom had always told me how smart I was, but now I felt like a robot. Do this! Eat that! Do as I say! Matron would hover, her hot breath close to my face, as she spoke harshly and with great authority no matter how minor the offence. Whatever she told me to do I did, but in my mind I pretended to be doing it my way. It was no victory at all, yet it gave me a fleeting taste of freedom.

I longed for real freedom. I could only imagine what it would be like to eat a banana whenever I wanted, or to have a large glass of milk. Or to eat a cookie or two just before bedtime, and not wake up in the middle of the night with my tummy growling. I'd go to sleep imagining a huge slice of warm, freshly baked bread covered with butter and homemade strawberry jam, and I'd pretend to eat it. I got to be so good at it I could feel it in my mouth, and even taste it too. Then I'd wake up starving, only to find some kind of hideous slop I was supposed to eat for breakfast.

After visits were moved to the mornings, my family only drove as far as the Kootenays on the Saturday, then stayed overnight with friends, usually Alex's or Connie's parents, and continued on to New Denver the next day. Sometimes when my folks stayed with Connie's our moms would go shopping together. And if they came on something they both liked, they might buy us matching outfits. That was really cute, but it meant Connie and I argued about what belonged to whom all the time. Once she took my black-and-white sweater and claimed it was hers.

"But it's not yours; it's mine!" I protested.

"No; it's mine!"

"Then show me the number in the collar."

"Don't need to!"

"Show me!"

"No!"

"Well, you don't need to show me, cause I can see it says eighty-five."

"You're wrong! It says fifty-eight."

"It's an eight and a five. That's eighty-five."

"It's fifty-eight. My mom does her numbers upside down."

"No one does numbers upside down."

"My mom does. It's so you can read it without having to take it off."

"You're crazy! It's eighty-five because it's got the line under it saying which way up it goes."

"No, my mom puts fifty-eight on my stuff with the line above it."

I wanted to punch Connie. Instead I just pouted. "I'm going to sit down right now and write a letter to my mom, and tell her not to buy the same clothes for us anymore when she and your mom go shopping!"

"Fine! But it's still my sweater!"

"Is not!"

"Is!"

"But look, that's an eight and a five…"

In all my time in New Denver I don't believe I ever did win an argument with Connie.

* * *

Soon summer came to an end. Leaves covered the ground in their glorious colours. The lake became soapy-looking and dirty, and debris started to accumulate. Halloween came, and we were told the gym would be available to us if we chose to have a party. I looked forward to these times. We didn't have a lot of joy in residence, so any time we could have a little fun I was always game.

Most of us had never been to a Halloween party before coming to New Denver, so we had no idea what to expect. But as we'd been invited to plan it we got together and started throwing ideas around. Members of staff helped with the decorating, so we hardly had to do anything in that regard. Our main concern was what we were going to go as.

"I know what I'm going to be," I gushed breathlessly.

"What?"

"Guess!"

"I give up."

"A gypsy!" The idea had been forming in my mind ever since we'd heard about the party. I had a skirt that was quite full and could easily pass for bohemian. Someone had lent me a blouse I could pull down on my shoulders, gypsy-style. I also had a beautiful scarf I could tie around my hair. I'm not sure where the jewelry came from but I borrowed necklaces, bracelets, earrings... and plenty of them! Prizes were to be awarded for the best costumes. I knew deep down that the first prize would be mine. All my friends agreed, so I believed I had it in the bag.

One of the girls from the annex was upset because she had no idea what to go as. I told her that because I had more than I needed I'd be glad to let her borrow some pieces. She accepted. When she was done she looked every inch a gypsy.

We walked over to the gym, took part in all the games, and had a great time. Looking at the costumes around me, I was confident I'd win first place. When it came time to announce the prize winners we all clustered round expectantly. To my utter dismay the other gypsy was awarded first prize. I couldn't believe it. I felt betrayed; after all, I was the one who'd lent her the costume! When my name wasn't called for second place I wanted to cry. I was sure I deserved that at the very least.

I told myself afterwards I'd learned a valuable lesson: don't lend your stuff to a competitor if you want to win first prize. But on reflection, I had to acknowledge that since most of the stuff I'd lent her wasn't even mine, I really wasn't in any position to complain!

* * *

We soon discovered that food handed over at the gate by our parents on visiting days often ended up on the matrons' table instead of getting to those for whom it was intended.

"Too bad there's nowhere to stash extra food, now we're not allowed to keep it in the lockers," I said one day.

An older girl overheard me. "Remember the Old Green Witch Lady?" she asked.

We all nodded. I was too frightened even to think about her, let alone talk about her.

"Well, she's not really a witch!"

"No?"

"No. She's really our friend!"

We all stared at her in amazement. "Friend?"

"But we've all heard the horrible stories about what she does to unsuspecting children!"

"That's just something we say so the matrons will never suspect what really goes on."

"It is?"

"So what does really go on?"

She looked around cautiously. We leaned in closer.

"She lets us store food in the root cellar in her back yard."

"She does that? Why?"

"She loves kids. And she feels sorry for us. She has friends who work in the kitchen and they've told her the sort of food they're ordered to prepare for us. She's really a very sweet old lady."

The girl took us over to the root cellar. We stared at rows of cardboard boxes with names in Russian printed on each box. There were no numbers. I could hardly believe our good fortune. Now we'd all be able to have our own secure stash of food from home.

"Does anyone ever steal other people's stuff?" I asked.

"If you see anything, let us know," she answered. "We'll deal with it."

As we turned to go, the girl stopped us. "But be careful not to let anyone see you going in or out of the cellar," she warned us, "or you'll be in big trouble! And so will the green lady."

We walked back to the annex in a daze.

"Cold varrenneki..."

"... pyrahi..."

"... chocolate cake..."

"... doughnuts."

Together we smacked our lips as we dreamed of endless supplies of the foods we most craved. It would be hard to overestimate the importance of our discovery that day. For the rest of our time in New Denver the food we stored in that cellar would liberate us from the choice of having to eat dormitory food or starving. We were eternally grateful for the opportunity to eat good home-cooked food on our way to and from school - and grateful to the sweet green lady for making it possible.

13. ENDURING THE MADNESS

Winter, 1956

When the first flurry of snowflakes appeared we looked forward to building the skating rink again. During the two or three days it took to get it ready I polished my skates, eagerly anticipating the enjoyment I knew lay ahead. Skating still gave me a sense of freedom that was unimaginable. With the benefit of the previous winter's experience I could now do all sorts of loops and twirls. I could even do complicated jumps, sometimes landing quite gracefully. To tell the truth, I'm not quite sure why I didn't end up with broken bones. I was a daredevil on ice, and loved to push my abilities to the limit. It seemed also that when I was participating in sports the matrons left me alone, and that too gave me a sense of freedom.

As my second Christmas in New Denver approached, our teacher announced that the school would be putting on an entertainment for the town. It was to be a mixture of concert and drama, with a little humour thrown in to round out the evening. I was so excited. I wanted to be one of the girls in a beautiful light blue dress and fancy hat carrying a parasol. I hoped I might get the chance to sing a bit, too. But no; Miss Spencer chose one of the other girls from the dorm to wear the frilly crepe-paper dress I'd set my heart on.

I swore quietly to myself. It was a devastating blow. The girl looked so beautiful in her costume, and I couldn't help wishing it could have been me on the stage instead of her. Her parasol looked as if it had been ordered from Eaton's catalogue, but I knew the teacher helped her make it.

I presumed I didn't get picked because my hair was so ugly. Instead, the teacher gave me the part of conductor for the kitchen rhythm band. I had to wear a huge chef's hat that kept sliding down because my ears weren't big enough to hold it up. I also had an oversized apron tied around my waist. That kept slipping, too. I'd wanted to look glamorous and instead I looked like a kitchen worker.

The band was kind of fun, though. We had spoons, pots and pans, a scrubboard, and some combs with paper folded over them. I swung a wooden spoon, and the first line of our song was 'Oh, we're the cookie kids with the kitchen rhythm band'. The kids who played the combs laughed because it tickled their lips. I think I did a good job, but my back was turned to the audience, so I couldn't tell if they really liked me or not. The drummer on the big pot was off the beat, so we got all mixed up, and the audience laughed. They didn't laugh at the girls in the blue dresses with the parasols though; they did everything perfectly. I decided that in future I'd hold out for a part I really wanted, and not let anyone push me into something I didn't want to do.

* * *

One day that winter when it was cold and rainy outside, Ruby and I were in the playroom. While we were running and laughing and generally doing what little girls do, the mailman came with some parcels. After he left, Mrs. Norton called us into the office. She'd been let go when the new director took over, and had later been re-hired as an assistant matron under Miss Crewell. Bitterness and resentment were now added to her naturally harsh temperament.

We were excited because it could only mean that one of the parcels was for us. My mom would sometimes send store-bought cookies, but what I loved most was her special doughnuts. Already I could feel the sugar on my lips. We ran to the office, our little faces filled with joy.

As soon as we walked in the door I could see Mrs. Norton wasn't pleased. I wondered whether my mom had written something in a letter to me she shouldn't have. The matrons read our mail and checked our parcels all the time.

"Hold out your hands," she said.

Ruby and I obeyed. But instead of giving us the expected letters, she reached for the razor strop behind her chair.

What's going on? I wondered. We hadn't done anything. We were just playing.

We were strapped, twice on each hand, with a flat razor strop. Mrs. Norton held it high over her head before bringing it down on my wrist. I could hear the whoosh of the strap but remained defiant, looking her right in the eye as she hit me. Once, twice. Then the other hand. It hurt like hell. My wrists were on fire and I could feel my breath being taken away, but I held back the tears and just kept staring. I didn't dare look down; I was sure I was bleeding to death.

And then it was Ruby's turn. Same thing, twice on each wrist. We were dumbfounded. We didn't cry, and didn't dare ask why the strap, for fear she'd just hit us some more.

"Running in the playroom is not allowed," she said. "Have you got that?"

Ruby and I looked at each other like Mrs. Norton was crazy. It's a play-room, right?

Yeah, we got it. Normally they never explained anything. But this time the explanation merely proved we were living in a world divorced from all reason.

We hurried to get outside and rub some snow into our wrists. Of course, a group of children had formed outside the door, waiting to see our reaction.

"How was it?" they asked.

I showed them my wrists. They were red and swollen, and tiny blood blisters were starting to form. I casually dropped the usual obscenities, and shrugged my shoulders.

The girls understood. They'd all had the strap at one time or another. Not a tear escaped either one of us, and that was a good thing. We still needed to let the kids know we were really tough. Being really tough was good, but it sure didn't stop the sting. I knew I'd feel it for days, and I did. So did Ruby.

* * *

I woke one morning with what felt like flaming footballs in my throat. I'd never felt such pain in my life. I went into the bathroom and the girls there just stared at me. I hardly recognized myself. My neck was swollen on both sides. I had no idea what it could be, but thought for sure I'd die before the day was out.

I went to the office and showed Miss Crewell.

"I'm sick! My throat..."

"Nonsense! You're fine."

"But my neck's really swollen. And I've got a fever."

"You'll feel better after breakfast."

The matrons may have looked like nurses with their crisp, white starched uniforms, but they were generally incapable of any compassion. They certainly didn't seem to realize when a child was truly ill.

"It's just I think I might be dying," I croaked.

"Just get ready for school."

I pulled some clothes on and staggered over to the dining hall. The sudden cold air was like sandpaper in my throat. I was starving, but couldn't think of trying to eat with my throat so sore, so I jammed my pockets full of breakfast. I did manage to drink something, which seemed to help a little, but not enough to make me feel better. So I went back to the annex and complained again.

"I really don't think I'll be able to go to school today."

"Of course you will. Run along now!"

"But it might be mumps!"

Some of the other children had had mumps. They said the mumps really hurt. But by now Miss Crewell was getting irritated.

"Do as you're told, and get ready for school!" she snapped.

So off I went.

I stumbled over the hard, frozen snow on my way to school. I tried without success to hide my tears, because I didn't want anyone to see. I was burning with fever, and felt I was going to throw up. On the incline to the main roadway some children approached me.

"Are you okay?"

Their concern only made me cry harder. There was nothing any of them could possibly do for me. I just had go to school, and see how I survived there.

Mr. Stickler was driving by in his car. He noticed I was crying, pulled over, and gestured me to come over to the car. "What's wrong?" he asked.

I took off my scarf, and pointed to my neck. "I'm sick."

He made me get in his car. I liked that, because it was toasty warm inside. He leaned into the back and checked my neck, then turned the car around and took me straight back to the dorms. He marched me inside, and then, to my astonishment, proceeded to give Matron heck for sending me out into the cold.

She apologized.

To him, not to me.

Then she and Stickler moved away a little. I could hear them whispering. When he'd left, she really let me have it. "Put your pyjamas on, and don't be such a crybaby!"

I did, gladly, hoping she wouldn't change her mind.

"And you can go to bed in the dorm. The pink room's for children who're really sick."

Because Matron was cranky for getting in trouble with Stickler, I was afraid she'd take it out on me. Fortunately I escaped the worst of her wrath, because when she came by with some aspirin and took my temperature she gasped it was so high. I was in bed for a couple of days. The other girls said I was lucky because I didn't have to go to school. I was brought a tray of food for each meal, and I didn't get in trouble if I didn't finish it, because I was sick. Hot liquids were fine, but I couldn't eat solid food because my throat was so raw. This was the only time in all of my years at New Denver that Stickler showed any kindness whatsoever towards me.

The pain gradually receded. It had been agony, but it was worth it to see Matron get into trouble. My only big fear had been that if a child happened to be in sick bay on visiting day her parents weren't allowed to see her. Even though sometimes I wished we didn't have visiting days because of the pain of separation afterwards, they were still my only truly happy times, even if it was for such a brief period.

I decided I might be a doctor when I grew up. I'd be very kind to my patients, not like the matrons.

* * *

One evening we were already in bed waiting for lights out when Miss Crewell decided to curl one of the girls' hair. She did this on a regular basis. She'd pick on girls who had the most beautiful hair and give them a hairdo, whether they wanted one or not. That night it was the turn of Myra, a quiet girl everybody liked. As she carefully arranged the bobby pins and curlers in Myra's hair Myra begged her to stop.

"I don't want my hair done!" she protested.

Miss Crewell ignored her. "Stop wriggling, child! How am I expected to do a good job if you keep wriggling?"

"But I like my hair the way it is."

"Nonsense! It'll be much more attractive this way. You'll see."

Myra started crying.

"Hold still!" Matron snapped at her.

Myra finally stopped pleading, but we could see the tears rolling down her cheeks as she sat in silence and allowed the hairdressing to continue. It took a long time, but it was important to Miss Crewell that every pinned curl be perfect. When it was done she admired her handiwork. "There! What did I tell you! You look very attractive now!"

And with a satisfied toss of her own permed and bleached hair, she turned and left the room.

Myra barely waited for the lights to go out before announcing in a whisper that she was taking the pins out. A few of us jumped on the bed and helped her, piling them neatly on her night stand. After a while Miss Crewell came back for a routine check. She saw with displeasure that Myra had no curlers in her hair.

"What's this?" she demanded, turning on the lights.

"They fell out, Miss Crewell. When I tried to lie down."

"Nonsense!"

"But it's my hair type! They come loose when I turn over."

Miss Crewell merely shook her head in disbelief that anyone could be so ungrateful, and proceeded to put them all back in. Myra protested, but she was no match for the matron.

As soon as the lights went out we watched as Myra pulled every pin curl out and threw them on the floor. Boy, was she ever going to get it! Matron came along and saw the pin curls. On went the lights, in went the pin curls. Out went the lights, out came the pin curls. I could see it would go on all night or until one of them gave in. Curls in, lights out. Curls out, lights on. We were giggling hysterically under our covers as the drama unfolded. Even Myra was struggling to keep a straight face as Matron finished resetting her hair one more time. This time though, Miss Crewell stopped in the doorway before turning out the light.

"Girls!" she said in a tone that brought silence to the room. "If the pin curls come out one more time, next visiting day is cancelled. Is that clear!"

The next morning the pin curls were still in Myra's hair. When she brushed it out it did look kind of pretty. We were proud of the little girl who defied authority, and she was a hero for quite a while.

"What the hell was all that about?" I asked later.

My friends looked at me as if I were dumb.

"You've been here this long and you still expect them to show reason?"

Actually, I was hoping that just once one of the matrons would put the pin curls in my hair, because I believed I still had the ugliest hair in the world. But I didn't dare ask for the pin curls, because then some of the girls would criticize me. Who knows, they might even have brought up the whole spy thing again. Our women never curled their hair, or wore make-up. Many never even wore a pair of pants. But already I was determined that when I grew up I'd perm and colour my hair, and put on tons of makeup. I'd give myself red, red lips, and wear the shortest skirt and the highest heels I could find. No one would recognize me.

I just had to wait about ten more years.

14. THE SMALLEST OF SMALL MERCIES
Spring, 1957

Visiting days came and went. We so looked forward to these visits, it would be hard to describe the feeling of anticipation. We prayed for our parents, that the drive up would be safe, and that ill health wouldn't prevent them from coming. I always tried to look my best, because I didn't want them to worry about me. My mouth would be watering long before visiting hour as I imagined my mother's borscht and pyrahi and varrenneki. I often felt guilty, longing for food instead of worrying how the visit would go.

We knew our parents were on the way when we could see the clouds of dust coming from the Cape. They parked all over the Japanese village, and then gathered together for the walk down to the dorm. The older girls provided the bread and salt and water, the simple necessities of life present at every Doukhobor prayer meeting. My dad had sculpted a dove out of wood, and that was placed on the table as well.

We'd begin with prayers. Then came the glorious singing as we heard our parents approach. The sound of our voices blending in harmony with theirs was like nothing on earth. It bound our souls together in a union of the spirit no caregivers could ever destroy. Some of the songs were specifically Freedomite songs, while others such as the Lord's Prayer, which we always sang, were from the wider Doukhobor tradition.

I kept my fingers crossed until I could see my mom. Then the joy of seeing her and the pain of not being able to touch her would hit me. Our parents would walk right up to the fence and stop, but the singing would continue. I remember thinking we shouldn't sing so long, that it took up too much of the visit.

After the hymns we'd all go to our regular places at the fence. From the moment the thermos was opened and I smelled my mother's hot borscht I'd eat until I thought I'd burst, knowing that unless some food was left at the green lady's house it would be another two weeks before I'd taste such wonderful food again.

It was rare for the entire family all to come on the same visiting day, but it did happen. By the entire family I mean my parents, my maternal grandparents, Auntie Vatkin, and of course my younger sisters. Of all these my Grandma Zebroff probably came the least frequently, because she was getting old and it was hard for her to travel. All my years in New Denver never warranted a visit from my father's parents, Mike and Helen Chernoff, in Saskatchewan. I was sorry they never came, because I would have been proud to introduce them to my friends. I was sure they wouldn't believe they were my kin. I don't recall any letters from them either, and my little heart was sad.

Whenever Kathrine and Marie visited, my parents usually wanted them to be inside the fence with me so I'd have someone I could kiss and hug. I really missed them, but as time went by I felt like asking my parents not to bring them. When I'd first arrived I was eight, Kathrine was six, and Marie was four. They were safe visiting then, because they were too young to be put in the dorms. As they grew older I found myself constantly looking over my shoulder, hoping the police guarding us wouldn't suspect my little sisters were of compulsory school age. There was very little the police could do to prove non-attendance at school on a Sunday, which is perhaps why my parents took the risk of bringing them. But I didn't think of that then. My heart was in my throat the whole time, fearing first Kathrine and then Marie would be detained, and I'd have the responsibility of looking after them.

The terror is hard to put into words, but as a child I remember the cold, sick feeling that would engulf me. I was already there. I knew the rules and regulations, what to do to keep out of trouble with the matrons. I knew the pecking order, and how to stay out of trouble with the other children. My sisters and I got along very well but I knew they wouldn't listen to me all the time. They were both feisty, full of life and laughter. That would have to be contained, for New Denver was serious business. My overactive imagination foresaw their lively spirits crushed by the unrelenting pain and confusion that awaited them.

Not that life was easy for them at home. Once when my mother and sisters were out a police car had come by. A neighbour said the police had rapped on the door for a long time, then walked around the house. They looked in the woodshed and the other outbuildings, including the outside toilet. Mom never let Kathrine and Marie hide there though, because it was too dangerous. The police called out a few times, and when there was no answer they left. Now when strangers approached the house my sisters would both hurry into the cellar just as the three of us had before. Since they might have to stay in there some time, Mom had taken to leaving a small lunch packed on the stairs.

"Sometimes mice find the lunch first, and there are bits eaten out of the sandwiches," Kathrine told me. "We sit there until Mom tells us the coast is clear."

"Sometimes we're hiding down there for hours!" Marie added.

"I wouldn't mind hiding all day," I said. "At least no one yells and screams at you."

"It's scary down there!"

"Maybe. But it would be peaceful."

I lived in fear in the dorm, and my sisters lived in fear at home. I envied them because they got to hug and kiss our parents, especially Mom, all the time, and eat good food. I'm sure they felt resentment towards me, because everything was being done for me, but they too were living disrupted lives. Their existence had become a game of hide-and-seek, only they were playing for keeps. They knew if they made a mistake they could be joining me behind the fence for good.

During bad weather we hung blankets over the fence to protect us from the wind and rain. This worked in summer, but when the fierce winds of winter were howling off the lake the blankets were no help at all. I'd be so cold my teeth were chattering. It was hard to carry on any sort of conversation with my thoughts distracted by the warm buildings behind us.

I longed for the touch of my family during visits, but the holes in the fence were only big enough to allow my fingers through. No matter how hard I tried I could never get my whole hand between the links. When I tried to kiss through our metal jail I could hardly feel whoever was on the other side. As fall turned into winter it got worse. When my mom tried to kiss me through the fence my skin froze to the chain-link, and my lips would chap and peel. It didn't stop me, because I wanted to kiss my mom more than anything, but it was a painful reminder of each visit. My lips looked awful all winter long because just as they started to heal the next visiting day would come around.

The police were always highly visible, and their presence was intimidating. I wondered why they had to be there. After all, we were just children. How much harm could we do? There were usually just three or four of them on duty after the fence went up. Sometimes they'd circulate among the families. I learned at the dorm to be fearful of the police, and this fear stayed with me until I was in my forties. I tried to believe they were just regular people, but many of the children at the dorm had very different stories about them. Some had been hunted down like wild animals, or had seen their parents brutally clubbed, and when that happens it's hard to attribute humanity to the person in the uniform. Even when we weren't being bad and a policeman came around, we'd avoid his gaze. Sometimes the police would follow particular children in their car as they went to and from school. I'm not sure what warranted this, but I suppose they were worried one of us might try to run away.

When the visit was over the blankets came down and my father packed them away. The family waved goodbye as they sang prayers and then walked up the incline to where their vehicles were parked. Despite the cold, most of us stood and waved as long as we were able to, until someone in authority made us go in. I knew my parents had a long journey ahead of them. The roads were pretty bad any time of year, but the Cape was treacherous in winter. I'd say a silent prayer after every visit that God would take care of my family and they'd get home safe and sound.

The time after visits was the worst. My heart would ache for my family, knowing I wouldn't see them for another two weeks. Sometimes I almost wished we didn't have visits, because they left me so upset. I thought it would be better never to see my family again rather than to keep going through such torture. I was always happy to see them, but even before the visit was over my heart would be breaking, knowing they'd be going home and leaving me behind. After each visit I'd lie in bed crying silent tears, feeling my mother's warm breath still on my cheeks, wishing with all my heart I could be at home with her and the rest of my family. The sense of loss would last for days. After two weeks of struggling to convince myself that I could cope on my own and that I didn't need anyone else, the next visiting day would arrive and the emotional turmoil would start all over again.

* * *

I was on my way out to breakfast one morning when Miss Crewell stopped me.

"Where are your overshoes, Helen?"

I was surprised by the question, but even more surprised when I looked in my slot and they weren't there.

"I don't know, Miss Crewell."

"And why not?"

Something about her tone made me nervous.

"I don't know."

She indicated a pair of overshoes lying on the floor. "Would those be them?" She knew of course before she asked that they were mine because they were marked with the number eighty-five.

"Yes, they're mine!" I said, seizing them and trying to get outside as quickly as possible. "Um, and thank you for finding them, Miss Crewell!"

"I wouldn't put them on just yet, Helen."

"No?"

"No. I'd like you to step into my office first."

My heart was thumping as she closed the door behind me. I knew I was in trouble, but how bad I couldn't yet tell.

"There are good reasons why we are expected to keep the dorms neat and tidy," she began. "Unfortunately, this is impossible with slovenly children like you who just throw their overshoes anywhere they please."

"But Miss Crewell, I always put my stuff where it belongs!" My mind was racing, desperate to figure a way out. "They must have been knocked accidentally! Maybe when one of the other children was getting theirs out."

She took a step closer, towering over me. "To see someone so consumed with her own self-righteousness that she's willing to pass the blame onto others rather than accept the consequences of her own thoughtless acts is appalling! It disgusts me! I look at you and my stomach actually heaves..."

She went on like this for some time. Miss Crewell strapped many, many boys and girls, and the story was always the same. She took pleasure in trying to make her victims feel worthless through psychological intimidation before imposing the punishment itself.

"If you're not going to obey the rules then the only course of action left open to me is to punish you."

My heart sank. Not just at the punishment itself, but also because the other girls would want to know what it was for, and the teasing and taunting could go on for days. I waited to hear what she had in mind. Extra chores? Kitchen duty? Mopping the floor?

When I saw her reach into the drawer for the strap I just about peed myself. No! Not the strap! Not just for my overshoes being on the floor! I'd heard all about the dreaded Crewell Straps. She'd swing with all her might, her arm bent almost to her back. And when the strap came down the whoosh preceded the pain by a second. Even the bigger boys said it hurt like hell, and some of them were twice my size and tough as old boots.

"But I do obey the rules, Miss Crewell. I do! All of them! Even the petty ones and the ones that don't make any sense!"

My pleading fell on deaf ears. "Put out your hands!"

I thought I was going to faint. I'd spent my days following the rules because I was so afraid of her. Now she was going to strap me, and I'd probably die from the blows. This would be my last day on earth. I'd never get out alive. One final thought flashed through my mind - I want my Mom!

As Miss Crewell lifted the strap, the breakfast bell rang. Irritation flashed in her eyes, but then an idea seemed to come to her. Her expression brightened, and she put the strap down.

"Go and eat," she said. "I'll deal with you later."

I grabbed my overshoes and hurried from the room as quickly as I could.

Connie, Irene, Anna and Natalie were waiting outside to look at my welts.

"So what happened?"

"Where are they?"

"She said she'd give it to me later."

I was trembling with fear as I walked over to the dining room. The girls looked at me with sad eyes. Many of them had felt the strap from Crewell before. It was one of the scariest things, far worse than no visiting or getting your mouth washed out with soap for speaking Russian.

I tried to eat my breakfast, but it wouldn't go down.

"I wish she'd just beaten me to death and got it over with," I said. I wrapped the food in paper, and stuck the bag in my pocket. "Now I'm going to have to live in fear until she gets me."

For the next few hours my heart pounded as if it were going to burst out of my chest. I tried to play with the other children but my mind was always on the fact that at any moment I could be called into the office to receive my punishment.

Lunch time came, and I dreaded going. I knew Crewell would be there. She was always one of the first members of staff to show up at mealtimes, because she loved to eat. To get into the dining room we had to walk up a flight of steps right by the window where the matrons sat. As I approached the steps I fell down on my belly and crawled up slowly as my friends kept an eye on the window. I made it in unseen, but then the fear was that Crewell would spot me over the pony wall and remind me to come into the office after lunch. For whatever reason, she didn't look for me. She was probably too busy stuffing her face with good food while we attempted to eat the slop before us. I thanked God that for the moment I was safe.

For the next few days I steered clear of her. Whenever Crewell approached, my friends signalled me and I'd run around the corner, crawl under the bed, hide in the shower - anything to get away from her. I never spoke or moved as long as she had an opportunity to notice me. I continued to crawl into the dining room for meals so that if she was sitting by the window she'd have no chance to see me and remember the strap. When days later I finally encountered her face to face, I put on my best 'what overshoes?' expression and hoped she couldn't hear my thumping heart.

I never did receive the strap from Crewell for the overshoe incident. I don't know if she forgot, or if she deliberately let me live in fear all that time. In the end I just thought she'd gone senile. I didn't mind. In the dormitory we were always grateful for whatever small mercies we could get.

* * *

Slocan Lake was a magnificent sight in the spring. On calm days the water was so blue it seemed that, like the sky, it could go on forever. At other times the wind picked up, and waves crashed white and angry against the cement walkway. The water was at its highest then, with logs and branches swept down from further up the lake. At school we played marbles in the muddy playground. I was good at it, and soon accumulated an enviable collection. I had a big steely, which had fallen out of my auntie's car and she'd let me keep it. I also had a huge cat's eye. I played for a long time to win it, and the loser cried.

As soon as the high water was gone, all the children were sent down to the beach to clear away the debris that had accumulated over the winter. We scurried like mice, picking up every piece of litter until the beach was spotless. We made a huge pile of the driftwood, and then had our first bonfire of the season. We sang and had marshmallows, and looked forward to warmer days.

One visiting day that spring a shadowy figure called Ivan moved cautiously among the families, speaking in Russian, so he wouldn't be overheard. He was well-known in the Freedomite community as someone with his finger on the pulse of what was going on.

"Good news," he said to me as he passed. "It looks like you'll be leaving soon."

"Really?" I was so overjoyed I could hardly speak. Those were the words I'd longed to hear ever since I'd arrived in New Denver. A torrent of emotions flooded my mind. I'd be able to hug my mother again! I'd be able to play with my sisters!

"Yes," he said. "We'll all be moving to Russia very soon."

"What?!" Russia?! I couldn't believe what I was hearing.

Russia???

How was that good news? I was Canadian. I didn't know anyone in Russia.

"It's true - a ship will come to the dorm and pick you all up."

"A ship? On Slocan Lake?" My head was spinning.

"It'll come right to the dorm. You'll get on it, and we'll all finally be free forever."

"When?"

"That's not been decided yet. But it will happen. You'll all have to be ready to drop everything and get on board at a moment's notice."

When we were alone the ship was a constant topic of conversation in the dorms.

"Why a ship? Why now?"

"It's because of the case," someone said.

"What case?"

"The Perepelkin case."

Not long before, the parents of one of the boys in New Denver had gone to court to get their son released. Their argument was that government policy regarding compulsory public education violated our religious principles. The case went all the way to the Supreme Court but was eventually rejected. It was after the loss of this case that Freedomite leaders started talking seriously about making plans to return to Russia, claiming we didn't have the religious freedom promised us in Canada.

When we discussed the plan later it didn't sound plausible.

"How will they get a boat up to the dorm? The water's too shallow on the beach, and probably at the wharf as well."

"Maybe we'll have to swim out to it."

I wasn't very happy about that. I could tread water pretty well, but I didn't see myself swimming out to any ship.

"Well, maybe they'll send lifeboats to pick up the kids who can't swim."

That sounded a lot more reasonable.

"But a bunch of kids in lifeboats would make a lot of noise. I'm sure the matrons would try and stop us."

"I'd bet if Tadi's on duty he wouldn't stop us."

* * *

We wondered who'd decided we'd be going to Russia. Most speculation pointed to Stephen Sorokin, our spiritual leader. I didn't know anything about him except that he lived in South America somewhere, but we figured nothing that important could happen without his approval. I had questions about him too. How come he lived so far away? The pastors in the local churches lived in town. I knew, because I'd been asking the non-dorm children in my class at school. We all had different opinions, but no one could really answer my questions.

We were repeatedly assured on many different visiting days that we'd all be going back to Russia, and very soon. So from then on we kept an eye on the lake as much as we could. I didn't like the idea at all, but I decided I'd keep my stuff together, just in case I had to leave quickly.

Thank God I speak Russian, I thought. And had made the decision to learn to read and write it as well!

Once, a couple of children were making plans to run away. We were all in favour of helping them, until someone remembered the ship.

"What if it comes when you're still on the road?" they were asked. "Then, even if you do get home, your parents might already be on their way to Russia."

They changed their minds then, and I was glad they did. My main worry was that they'd get eaten by wild animals in the forest between New Denver and home.

I don't know if I really believed a ship would come and get us. I'd never heard of a ship going from the ocean onto a lake. It would make more sense for us to drive first to Vancouver and get on a boat there, and then sail to Russia. But why would our parents lie to us? And I didn't want to move to Russia, anyway. I didn't know much about the place except that it was very cold, and very far away. Why would anyone want to go back there?

My Grandma Zebroff used to tell us stories about how hard it was living there when she was a little girl. Georgians and Armenians used to raid the villages, kidnapping children. A crier would run through the village screaming for people to hide. Did our parents really not remember all this? *Maybe I should remind them next visiting day,* I thought. Or maybe Ivan was lying to us, so that none of us would try to run away. Somehow that made more sense to me. I wondered if Auntie Vatkin was planning on going to Russia. Maybe she'd let me live with her if she wasn't. And my grandparents were getting old. Maybe if they didn't go I could live with them.

I hated having to think so hard all the time.

15. CRUEL SUMMER

Summer, 1957

Our swimming instructor that year was very handsome. His name was Archie Howard and he looked like a college man. Archie had dark hair and nice eyes, and immediately became known as Hondo, after the ruggedly handsome cowboy played by John Wayne in a movie we saw that year. The younger girls from the annex just thought he was good-looking, but lots of the older girls from the dorm fell in love with him. Some of them offered their services to help demonstrate mouth-to-mouth resuscitation for the benefit of the other girls in swim class. All that summer we heard reports of fights among the older girls because each of them thought Hondo liked her best.

I loved swimming. We all did. When classes were over we generally played in the water as long as we were allowed. Connie in particular spent hours in the water. In her usual way she'd be oblivious to everything going on around her. She liked to submerge herself until only her eyes and nose were visible, and then calmly snorted through her nostrils to create bubbles on the water. When she closed her eyes, surely envisioning a world far different from the one we were in, she looked like a frog. I'd have to get close to her and yell almost in her ear before she'd notice me. Sometimes I'd sneak up on her and watch the patterns her breathing made on the surface of the water. I always wondered how she could be so still when her feet weren't touching the bottom of the lake.

The swimming area was surrounded by a rope boom, and we weren't allowed beyond it. We liked to swim out to the raft, where the water was deep, and then jump off. We'd swim underwater into the forbidden area, and when we surfaced on the wrong side of the boom our excuse was always, 'Got turned around. Sorry!'

From time to time that summer we'd have a campfire in the evening. We'd gather dry wood from the beach or from the dormitory grounds, and then the swimming or gym instructor would light the fire. If the instructor was Archie, the older girls would push and shove to try and sit next to him. On those occasions we'd sing a few Russian folk songs; not many, but we did sing in both languages. After a while whoever the instructor was would usually start singing 'Ninety-nine Bottles of Beer on the Wall'. It was one of their favourites, but I was never comfortable with it because as Doukhobors we weren't supposed to drink, so I thought we probably shouldn't sing about it either. I could never have convinced the older girls though. They were too busy trying to get into the good graces of Hondo. As I loved singing I generally joined in eventually, but I felt really naughty. I could only imagine the look on my grandfather's face if he were to hear me.

Archie was a good instructor, and most of us learned to swim well. He didn't yell much, but he drove us very hard. We often had to keep going until we were ready to drop. I wanted to learn, so I didn't complain. Ever since I'd discovered we might have to swim out to the boat that would come for us I'd decided to work hard to improve my technique. I figured I could swim most of the way out doing breast stroke, and then maybe switch to back stroke when I got tired. I may not have wanted to go to Russia, but I sure didn't want to get left behind either.

* * *

The greatest tragedy at New Denver occurred during that second summer, while I was still in the annex. Early one morning Miss Crewell tiptoed into the room while we were all still in bed. I was awake, so I heard her, but I made no sound. Miss Crewell usually frowned or scowled, but that morning she seemed genuinely upset. I knew straight away something really bad must have happened. I always worried about how everyone was at home, especially my two little sisters, so when Matron continued past my bed I found myself dizzy with relief.

She stopped at Myra's bed and woke her up. Sleepy-eyed, Myra asked her what she wanted. For the first time since I arrived I detected a hint of tenderness in Miss Crewell's voice as she asked Myra to come into the office. The next thing I knew, the whole dorm woke in confusion to hear Myra screaming that she wanted to know what had happened to her mom.

Someone overheard Miss Crewell tell Myra that her mother had died. Apparently, Miss Crewell actually tried to put her arms around Myra. She wouldn't tell her any details though, only that Myra was to pack up her belongings and get ready to go home.

When Myra came out of the office we tried to comfort her, but she was crying so hard she could barely get any words out. I'd never seen anyone cry like that before. We didn't know how to deal with it at all. We all cried, we all hugged and held each other and tried to offer comforting words, but I understood that for Myra my words were meaningless. All she wanted was to be with her mother, and she would never see her again, or hold her close, or be hugged and kissed by her.

Oh how my heart ached for Myra, and I could do nothing for her!

None of us knew what would happen to her. Would she be allowed to go home for the funeral? I wondered who'd come to visiting hours. We all knew how hard it was to see our moms just twice a month; none of us could imagine never seeing our mom again.

In a very short time, Myra was taken from the annex. We never saw her again.

Over the following days we talked about nothing but the tragedy. We didn't know what had happened, and we couldn't understand why no one was telling us. When I questioned any of the matrons none of them would explain the tragedy. I asked but no one had any answers. I understood about death. Like the other children I went to funerals from the time I was very young, although the shocking finality of death never fully registered until this happened. What I couldn't understand was the secrecy. Why, why, why?

Gradually the news came in letters from home that Myra's mother had committed suicide. Oh, those words were so hard for us children to understand! That she had killed herself because she couldn't bear the pain of separation from her child anymore sent a chill through my soul. On visiting day we learned more details. We heard about how big and beautiful her funeral was; many people had come to say goodbye. We all prayed for Myra and her family. We came to believe that Myra's mom loved her so much she would rather die than live without her little girl. But we were still all extremely upset - not just thinking about poor Myra, but wondering if any more of us would go home to bury a parent.

Every night I prayed fervently to God that my mom would be okay. I pictured my mother's beautiful sad face, so soft and understanding. She always looked lately as if her eyes were on the brink of tears. Then I imagined myself in Myra's situation, and I felt my heart would break. I knew if anything happened to my mom I'd want to die myself.

O dear God, please don't let my mom die! I prayed. *Make her strong! I love her so much!*

I had to be doubly sure now never to tell how bad it was in the dorm in case that made my mom worry more about me - and then maybe do something rash. I promised myself I'd tell her it was okay there, that I was used to it by now. I knew how much my mom loved me. Would she decide to end her life?

Please God, don't let my mom love me as much as Myra's mom loved her!

Those days were traumatic not only for myself but also for many other children. I'd lie in bed and wonder if it wouldn't be better for Myra to come back to New Denver; then she'd miss her mom the same as always and the only time it would really be upsetting would be when we'd have visiting day and her mom wouldn't be there. Otherwise she'd be just like the rest of us, living there without our parents.

I was afraid to tell my idea to anyone in case they thought I was crazy.

* * *

At one point two of the older girls from the dorm, aged fourteen or fifteen, had made a successful escape. We heard later they'd hopped a garden wall, and had pretended to be weeding a vegetable patch along with some older women when the police asked about them. I don't recall any response from the authorities, although we talked amongst ourselves about how brave the girls were. The road from New Denver was all mountain terrain, long and hazardous. But they got away, and were never brought back.

Inspired by their example, another of the older girls and her brother decided the lake was their way to freedom. They clambered onto an old log that had washed up on the shore, and made a break for it using flat sticks as oars. They were moving pretty fast. We figured they'd be in Slocan Park in a day or two.

The alarm was raised, and the swimming instructor was sent out in a canoe to bring them back. The wind picked up, waves crashed over them, and they were blown back to shore while the instructor watched. I felt bad for them because they sure got it from Matron, and then from the director. On top of that they lost visiting privileges as well.

* * *

Summertime in New Denver was beautiful. When we weren't swimming or doing chores, Irene and I loved to get away from the Dorm and explore the surrounding area. In our wanderings we'd discovered a meadow area way up on the mountainside. It was an idyllic alpine setting, green and peaceful with a magnificent view of the lake. Since it was also about as far as we could get from the dorm and still be back in time for the next mealtime, the sense of freedom we felt there was intoxicating.

Best of all, wild berries grew there. We knew that when they were in season we could go there and stuff our faces with wild raspberries, strawberries and salmonberries. Sometime we'd find huckleberries, and they were the treat of treats - big, beautiful, luscious, juicy, and dark, dark blue.

One gloriously sunny day we decided to go up there. It was a long hike up the steep mountain slope, but we had all afternoon so we just walked and talked. When we finally got there, oh, the berries! They were delicious! We forgot our cares as we laughed and picked berries and stuffed ourselves. We ate and ate as we ran from bush to bush. Oh how we ate! We were always hungry, so this was like heaven for us.

When we'd eaten so much fruit our bellies hurt, we lay on the wild grass and talked. Then we fell silent, and each daydreamed about being at home with our family. A gentle breeze played around us, and the sun warmed our limbs. Way below us Slocan Lake was a large, brilliant blue, and the sunshine glistened off it. Bees hummed and birds sang. My eyelids felt heavy.

Irene was the first to speak. "Wouldn't it be great if it could always be like this?"

I was preparing to murmur a drowsy assent when all of a sudden our blissful day was shattered by the wail of the dormitory horn.

It could happen at any time, the horn. It would sound, and we were given just a few minutes to be standing straight and tall at the foot of our beds for a head count. They did it quite often when we had a break from school. There was no rhyme or reason to it; it just happened, and always came when we least expected it.

We leapt to our feet at once, and took off for the dorm as if our lives depended on it. There was no time to use the path; we cut in a straight line down the mountainside. We tripped, we stumbled, we snagged our clothing as we ran through shrubs and leapt over branches. We ran like the devil himself was behind us, for in fact that wasn't far from the truth. It was the fear of punishment that propelled us down the mountain at such a breakneck speed. The one most dreaded, of course, was no visiting day. That punishment hung over us every second of every day.

I tripped and fell down and got pieces of grit stuck in my knee. Irene fell also, and her leg started to bleed. We helped each other up, shrieking encouragement at one another to go faster, faster.

At the foot of the mountain there was a cleared slope strewn with the stumps of felled trees. In winter, the stumps were buried by snow and we used it as a slide. But this was summer, and everything was exposed. We launched ourselves onto the slope, landing on our backsides and sliding down through the dirt and the stumps and rocks and gravel. The punishment for ripping our jeans wouldn't be as severe as being late for the horn. One of my shoes fell off. I didn't bother to put it back on. I just grabbed it and ran.

We sprinted the rest of the way to the annex, totally out of breath. Irene gasped in surprise as we burst into the room.

"They haven't started yet!"

Sure enough, as I tumbled in behind her I saw everyone standing beside their beds with their feet together, arms at their sides, backs straight as an arrow - and Matron, with her clipboard and wristwatch and pencil, poised to seal our doom.

We'd made it! I'm still not sure exactly how, but there we were, scratched and bruised and standing to attention beside our beds.

Matron could tell at a glance who was there, and worse, who wasn't. She took a quick look, then did the roll-call. She always called our names out in alphabetical order. Since my last name was Chernoff, it came too close to the beginning for comfort. I often wished my name could have started with a Z, like my grandparents', if only to give me the advantage of a few extra seconds at moments such as this. I stood by my bed, shoe in hand, looking like a rag doll, and responded when my name was called. Irene and I were grinning like a couple of monkeys; we were covered in dirt and blood and berry juice, but we'd made it!

The matron on duty that day was in a good mood, and merely scolded us for our torn clothing, though we always lived in fear that she might one day decide to punish us for yesterday's sins.

It was worth it though. The berries were the best I'd ever tasted!

16. SIMMERING REBELLION

Fall, 1957

"What a bitch!"

"There's no reasoning with her."

"She needs to be taught a lesson!"

A bunch of us were grumbling at the latest injustice inflicted by Miss Crewell. She'd disciplined us for 'unruly behaviour.' I don't even remember the reason now, but the punishment was to withdraw visiting privileges from all girls in the annex for one visiting day.

"I wonder what'd happen if we beat her up?" one of us wondered out loud. "You know, got her from behind so she couldn't see who was doing it to her."

"You can't do that!" someone gasped.

"Why not?"

"We're Doukhobors. We're pacifists!"

"But she's really gone too far this time! We have to do something to stop her."

"Yes, but..."

"If we don't stand up for ourselves, who will?"

"And who knows what'll happen next?"

Not mentioned, but in all our minds, was the recent tragedy. Resisting the matrons was no longer a matter of patiently enduring abuse. It had become a matter of life and death.

"Well, what are our options?"

"We could put pins on the ends of her binoculars."

"We could slip a tarantula under her covers."

"We could stitch open her eyelids and leave her staked to an ant hill."

Watching Saturday movies had taught us many sick and imaginative ways to take revenge, not excluding death.

"No, seriously."

Alex too disliked Miss Crewell. He came up with a great idea. "How about we make her have an accident so she has to take time off?"

"Sounds good. How would that work?"

Alex explained his plan. Miss Crewell lived in her apartment in the annex, so she was always there. He suggested we get together late one night, when she'd be snoozing in her apartment instead of keeping watch.

"We go into the pink room, and we turn the floor polisher on end," he said. The pink room was where they stored the ironing board, a few mops and brooms, the sick beds for when a child required isolation, and of course the floor polisher.

The forty-ton floor polisher.

"Um... how would we do that?"

"We'd get some boys to help."

"But wouldn't it be too heavy even for them?"

"We'll find a way, okay!"

"Okay. Then what?"

"We prop it, heavy end up, against the door."

"The door that opens into the playroom?"

"Right. The only door there is in the pink room. Then one of us screams from inside the room."

"What sort of a scream?"

"A holler for help, I don't know!"

"Sort of, 'Aaarrrgh!!!?'"

"Something like that. Anyway, someone screams from the pink room. Crewell hears the cries of distress, and comes to investigate."

"And then...?"

"When Matron opens the door, the polisher falls forward onto her and gives her a bonk on the head that knocks her out. Possibly for good. Our prayers are answered, the bully of bullies is no more, and all our problems will be over!"

"Perfect! But wouldn't that kill her?"

"Maybe. But if it did..."

"But that's murder!"

"Not if we don't intend it."

"But we do intend it!"

"There's always the outside chance it wouldn't totally kill her. And don't forget how mean she is!"

We all knew our lives would be so much better if she weren't there. But I'd never have thought of us seriously contemplating murder.

"What's happening to us? We used to spend our time just trying to figure out how to run away and not get caught. Now we're planning ways to murder the matron. This place frightens me."

* * *

For the next few days we discussed the scenario endlessly.

"What if it hurts her but doesn't kill her? Just makes her really mad?"

"She'd probably kill us."

"We'd definitely lose all our visiting privileges."

"It's not worth taking the chance."

"You're right. We're better off killing her outright."

"It just seems like such a big step. Couldn't we just write a letter to someone? Tell them what it's like in here?"

"They've already tried that."

It was true. Our parents had protested conditions to everyone from the local magistrate to the premier of British Columbia. They'd even appealed to the United Nations. My mom had taken part in protests organized by mothers with children in New Denver. They'd travelled to Nelson, to Victoria, to Vancouver. Nothing had changed.

"So we're agreed? She has to go?"

What we were proposing was daunting. It might not even work. But we also knew it might be the only opportunity we'd ever have to assert ourselves, overthrow our oppressor and determine our own destiny.

"So are we doing it?"

We sized one another up, now no longer just friends, but co-conspirators. If we didn't even try, we'd have no one to blame but ourselves.

"Let's do it!"

* * *

At the end of the summer the director announced that sending food parcels to children through the mail would no longer be allowed. From then on the only remaining channel for delivery of food was through staff at the gate on visiting day. As food handed over didn't always make it to the child it was intended for, our parents' sole reliable option now was to leave food in the green lady's cellar, for their children to collect later.

By now I was quite familiar with the green lady. She was of medium height, and quite round. Her hair was gray and wispy, and fell around her face in little curls. I can still picture the warts on her face, but can't be sure there were any in reality. She always wore a green sweater, hence the name. Some of us thought her complexion was kind of green too, but again, that may just have been in our overactive imaginations. She was very quiet. I did meet her a couple of times, and even though I knew I was safe, I was still immature enough to shudder with fear.

* * *

The schoolchildren from town helped keep us abreast of current fashions. Saddle oxford shoes were the big trend one year. Some of the girls actually had a pair. Those of us who didn't were green with envy. Another time, pleated plaid skirts were very much in style. I begged Mom to make one for me. "A beautiful, burgundy-coloured one! Oh, please Mom! Please!"

Then one visiting day, to my surprise, my mother produced exactly the skirt I'd been dreaming of. She held it up for me to see through the fence. It was the most gorgeous piece of clothing I'd ever seen in my life. She'd even lovingly embroidered the number eighty-five into the waistband. I could hardly wait to wear it.

Then she handed it over to someone at the gate.

I saw the skirt a few days later. The daughter of one of the matrons was wearing it in school. I went up to her. "You're wearing my skirt!"

She denied it. "My mom bought it for me in Nelson."

I demanded to see the inside of the waistband. The girl didn't want to show me at first, but when a group of us approached her she let me see.

My heart sank.

There were no numbers there. But I could see the fraying where my mother's stitches had been taken out.

"What's the matter with these people?" I burst out. "Did no one ever teach them manners?"

"That's just the way things are," Anna said. "They steal our language, our heritage, our culture - and now our clothes."

Every time I saw that girl wearing the skirt my mother had sewn for me, I wanted to cry. I wanted to rip the skirt right off her, and leave her standing there with her underpants showing. I never did, though. Instead I just cried the silent tears that were such a part of life since my arrival in New Denver.

* * *

We discussed endlessly the pros and cons of assassinating Matron with the floor polisher, knowing there'd be no going back once we'd performed such an evil deed. Oh, how we wanted to be rid of her!

We hesitated partly because as Doukhobors we were strict pacifists, but also because of the fear of far worse punishment than even the matrons could dream up.

"We'd be laying ourselves open to the wrath of God, which would surely descend on us for our sin if we were to go ahead."

We all nodded sadly.

"Besides, we're not murderers."

We all agreed, again sadly.

"And even though Matron's really, really mean, it's still better to accept punishment from her for a short time than the wrath of God for ever and ever."

So we never did harm her, or anyone else for that matter. Instead, we chose to take a more subtle approach.

We children did the cleaning, and Miss Crewell's rooms had to be kept in tip-top shape at all times. We decided that from then on, whoever cleaned her apartment would move things around, hide things, generally do things to make her think she was losing her mind so she could be replaced by someone who had human emotions.

Our childish imaginations continued to run wild as to what kind of vengeance we'd like to wreak should we ever have her in our unfettered power, but for the time being we limited ourselves to hiding her keys, putting the dishes away in the wrong place, and doing other things just this side of naughty. When questioned, we'd lie through our teeth.

"Helen, did you switch the cushions on the chesterfield?"

"No, Miss Crewell."

"I spent an hour trying to get the radio to work this morning. Why is it unplugged?"

"I have no idea, Miss Crewell."

"And why is there a bowl of uncooked macaroni in the fridge?"

"Are you sure you didn't put it there yourself, Miss Crewell?"

* * *

I enjoyed all kinds of sports. I loved the exhilaration of running and getting lots of exercise. Outdoors I played baseball in the summer and skated on our home-made rink in the winter. Indoors, I played basketball and volleyball and all kinds of other games in the gymnasium. I always wanted to be on the same team as Anna, Natalie, Connie and Irene. We'd try to figure out ways not to be picked by the captain of any team we didn't want to play on. We'd hide behind other players until it was time for our chosen team's turn to pick. Then we'd leap out, yelling "Me! Me! Pick me!" As children we were like rubber balls. When we were playing sports, you could always hear a lot of laughter. I guess we'd all forget where we were. Sometimes in the middle of a laugh, a yearning so deep and so strong would come over me, and I'd just want to run out to the highway and keep running, never looking back, until I reached home.

We had special gym instructors at the dorm. Some were okay, but others were meaner even than the matrons. One of these was Mr. Corrigan. He looked oriental, though none of us were quite sure of his origins. Speculating on his parentage was a popular pastime among many of the children in the dorm. He was a tall, muscular man, and I jumped to attention whenever he entered the room. His word was law, and when he spoke we'd damn well better be listening, especially when he was laying down rules. He didn't need an excuse to punish us, and if he was ever caught hurting us he'd just blame it on the rough game we were playing. I usually tried my best to stay in his good books.

One day, some of us were standing around waiting to play basketball when he started explaining the rules. As I already knew how to play basketball I turned around to one of my friends and started talking. I got carried away, and never heard him tell me to be quiet.

Suddenly my head exploded.

The next thing I knew, I was lying face-down on the polished hardwood floor of the gym with stars careening around me. My face felt like it was on fire, my whole body throbbed with pain, and there was a horrible ringing in my ears. I tried to sit up, but thought I'd throw up or pass out if I did. Looking up, all I could see was a wall of girls stunned into silence. I couldn't figure out what had happened to me. I tried to mouth the question, but nothing came out, and no one replied.

Then I saw the basketball roll past.

Everything hurt and I could hardly breathe, but eventually I crawled up into a sitting position. Facing me I saw the huge, hairy legs of Mr Corrigan. For a second I thought he was going to help me get up on my feet again. But he didn't. Instead, he stood towering over me like a mountain.

"Get the hell up, and pay attention!" he yelled down at me.

I slowly got up, still confused, trying to figure out what was going on.

"And let this be a lesson to all you yappy girls," he snarled. "Next time I'll aim better and hit harder! I don't have all day to go over the rules! And just where do you think you're going?" This last remark was barked at me as I slowly started limping my way to the bench.

"I'm a bit dizzy. I need to sit down."

"I don't care how you feel. You're playing. Now!"

"But I'm hurt!"

"Now!"

I wanted to lash out at him and yell and scream, but knew it would do no good. Instead, I allowed murderous thoughts to run through my mind. *If only I was just a little bit bigger,* I thought, *I'd kick his ass up his throat. I'd beat the hell out of him. I'd make him chew the basketball and swallow the pieces.* For that I'd gladly take whatever punishment they chose to give me.

That of course never happened, as I was eleven years old at the time and weighed barely eighty pounds.

He made me play a game of basketball. I was surprised I could even move, but I did. Not too well, but I managed to get through it. The stars slowly disappeared and the pain eventually went away, but I felt like I'd been run over by a truck. I guess he was lucky he didn't kill me, because the force with which the basketball hit my head could have knocked a grown man to the floor.

I knew it would do no good to complain, for no one ever listened. We just had to survive whatever way we could.

* * *

One day, to my surprise, Mrs. Armstrong took Ruby and me aside as we were coming back from breakfast. "I'd like to invite the two of you to a birthday party next Tuesday," she said. "My daughter Margaret is turning eleven, and she asked if you could come."

"We'd love to!" I gushed. I could hardly believe our good fortune.

"Thank you, Mrs. Armstrong," Ruby said, "but I'm not sure we can."

"What!" I was horrified. I couldn't believe she was turning down the opportunity to go to a party with one of our school friends from town!

"Don't worry," Mrs. Armstrong said with a smile. "I've cleared it with the matron on duty."

"No, it's not that."

"What then?"

Ruby shuffled uncomfortably. "We'd like to give Margaret a gift, but we don't have anything."

"That's very thoughtful, Ruby, but it's really not necessary. I know Margaret would be happy just to see you there."

"I know, but I don't think we'd be able to enjoy ourselves if we didn't bring a gift."

"I understand."

"Why did you say that?" I demanded when we were out of earshot. "Do you go to so many parties that now you can pick and choose?"

"You know what the town kids say about us behind our backs," Ruby retorted. "I don't want to give them an excuse to think it's true!"

Before we left for school Mrs. Armstrong slipped some money into Ruby's hand. "Perhaps you can find a little something in town this weekend?" she smiled. "See you on Tuesday!"

* * *

The party was unbelievable. Oh my goodness, there were so many children! Everyone was happy. The laughter rang through the whole house. Oh, how

I danced and laughed! I felt like Cinderella in a fairy tale. The food was delicious, just like at home. Every bite I took was heaven, and I could eat as much as I wanted. I ate as I played the games with the other children, my hands full of cookies and goodies.

Ruby and I enjoyed every single moment. My heart was happy, my tummy was full, I played every game that was offered, and for the first and only time in New Denver I forgot for a few hours where I was, and the painful circumstances of why I was there. The children from town treated us with a kindness I wasn't used to, and I made up my mind to be much nicer to them from then on. And when the games were over and our tummies hurt from all the food and the laughter, Mrs. Armstrong brought us back to the dorm.

That party is etched in my memory for all time. When I remember it I can still see the face of Mrs. Armstrong, encouraging me to eat and drink, the smile on her face growing wider and wider. She was the best matron in New Denver by far. It was because she had so many children herself that she knew how to get things done without threats or yelling.

17. THE SMALLEST OF SMALL TRIUMPHS
Winter, 1957 – Spring, 1958

In December of 1957, a delegation of four men left for Russia to discuss with the Soviet government the possibility of the Freedomite community emigrating there, and to look for properties that might be suitable for us if we were to go. They received an official send-off from the community in Krestova. My father was one of the men selected to go.

I'm not sure why Dad was chosen to go to Russia. However the other three men who went with him had been very regular visitors at our home in Grand Forks when I still lived there. He was away for less than two months, but I remember praying for his safety every single night. I had a deep-rooted fear that he'd like it in Russia and decide not to come home.

While he was away I recall standing on the dormitory grounds, staring out at the water and waiting for the ship to appear on the lake so we could all board and go to Russia. I wondered often what life would be like in our homeland. I was a third generation Canadian, but I'd been conditioned to believe that Mother Russia was our real home, and it wouldn't be long until we all went back. Although the Cold War was then at its height, I don't recall any fears that Russia was going to bomb us. I'm sure we all thought that Russia knew where we were and would leave us alone.

While my father was away that winter, my sister Kathrine turned eight and became eligible to be taken to New Denver. From then on my parents would allow only Marie to come behind the fence, on those occasions when Kathrine did visit. Marie didn't like being sent into the dormitory grounds on her own, even with me to hold her hand. She wriggled and protested, and clung to my mother's skirt, the fear evident in her eyes. But my parents wanted me to have someone to hold, and she would eventually be sent in despite her protests.

Many times Kathrine stayed home in Grand Forks, and it would be a long time between visits for us. I missed her very much, for the three of us were very close.

Throughout my time in New Denver the speaking of Russian was strictly forbidden. We weren't allowed to use it at any time around the dorm, even after we'd all learned to read, write and speak English. We always spoke it amongst ourselves though, usually under our breath so we couldn't be heard. The matrons didn't catch us very often, but those who were caught had their mouths washed out with soap. This rule was strictly enforced at all times but especially after visiting days, when the awareness of just what it was we were being deprived of was most strongly on our minds. One particular day we were told once again that no Russian would be permitted. Our response was not to speak at all. When Matron spoke to anyone, we ignored her as though we were all deaf. Or we'd turn towards her, but not say a word. Needless to say, she wasn't amused.

We quickly learned how to use Russian without getting into trouble. Someone pointed out that the rule said we couldn't speak in Russian, but it didn't say anything about not singing in Russian. So we decided that for the rest of the day, whenever we communicated as we played or did our chores, it would be in Russian and it would be in song. We used a few traditional melodies we were all familiar with, but instead of the usual words we made up our own. One of us would sing a few lines and someone else would answer as if joining in the same song. No doubt Matron thought we were just singing old Russian folk songs when in fact we'd be singing things like "If she's so clever how come she's working as a matron in New Denver?" or "When I get out of here I'll..." followed by whatever fantasy most appealed to us - or sounded most ludicrous - at the time. It also came in handy when we needed to warn each other of Matron's approach.

We carried on conversations in this way throughout the day, singing, singing, singing. I remember singing of my longing to go home, and how terribly I missed my parents and my sisters. That my heart was breaking and that there were hardly any tears left.

The tune was always kind of the same, and Matron smiled as we took turns singing what we felt. It may be that she didn't particularly like us singing in Russian but tolerated it because she thought it meant we were happy and less likely to get into mischief. The trick, of course, was never to allow the slightest trace of a smirk to cross our faces, or Matron would know something was up and we'd all be in trouble.

We were smug, thinking we'd pulled a good one, but looking back I wouldn't be surprised if Matron knew exactly what was going on and chose not to do anything about it. Or perhaps we really did score one small success in our constant struggle for survival.

* * *

All through January and February of that winter I received postcards from my father showing images of exotic buildings, landscapes and people. I could only dream what it would be like to be over there with him. Lunch in Paris? The ballet in Moscow?

Finally, one visiting day, there he was. I was so excited to see him.

"Well, we did it!" he said, grinning with boyish enthusiasm. "We found some land that looks promising, and we've applied to the Soviet government for permission to move there!"

"That's great, Dad. Where is it?"

"It's in the Altai region."

"Huh?"

"Southwest Siberia."

"Siberia. That's cold, right?"

"Yup. Just like Canada. And you know what? I think they just might take us!"

Although I was still young my mother had home-schooled me well. I knew that the Soviet Union was officially atheist, and that it was routinely criticized by Western nations for its persecution of religious groups. I didn't think there was a chance in hell they wouldn't jump at the opportunity to make political capital out of a religious community from Canada seeking asylum within their borders.

"Yes, Dad, I guess they just might."

My father was a very large man who didn't say a whole lot, but this day was special, and he talked and talked. Oh, the stories he told were wonderful! Then he reached into his pocket and pulled out a package wrapped in tissue paper.

"Here's a little something I thought you might like," he said, pushing it through a square in the chain link fence. "I bought it for you in Paris."

My heart skipped a beat. While my Auntie Vatkin loved to buy us things when she could, presents from my parents were rare. We were quite poor, as were most of the families with children in the dormitories, so a gift other than a necessary piece of clothing was an absolute luxury. I unwrapped the present with trembling hands, and squealed with delight as I glimpsed a shimmer of silk. I opened it up and gasped as I saw that the gift my father had brought me from Paris was a beautiful silk scarf. It was long and thin, gradually fading from a dark red to white, and covered with little gold circles. Pinned to the scarf was a large peacock brooch, green with gold flecks. I'd never seen a gift like it in my life.

After visiting hour I ran through the different rooms, showing my scarf to anyone who'd stop and look. The other children were in awe of it. They all wanted to touch the gold circles and feel the silk. I let the girls drape it over their shoulders, put it on their head, tie it around their waist.

Imagine! Having something from Paris! We felt so glamorous and so grown up.

I rarely wore this treasure, but kept it wrapped in its tissue paper in the little drawer beside my bed. I'd take it out quite often and just look at it. My imagination soared as I caressed it with my cheek and recalled those magical words I'd heard from my father's lips: 'I bought it for you in Paris.'

* * *

Most of us accepted our lot in life, having grown accustomed to the rules and regulations. There were some though who were defiant to the bitter end. And, for us in the dormitory, the bitter end was always losing visiting privileges.

Some of the problems in the dorm were made worse by personality conflicts, and in such cases the matron would often become as childish as the youngster she was tormenting. One day Doris was mopping the floor in the girls' bathroom. Miss Crewell came by and complained about the way the job was being done.

"You're leaving too much water on the mop," she said. "You're not wringing it out properly. If you put that much water on the floor it'll lift the edges of the linoleum!"

Doris had heard it all before, so she rolled her eyes in frustration. At that, Miss Crewell began yelling and giving her hell. I guess Doris had heard all that once too often too, because she grabbed the heavy mop full of dirty water and swung it straight into the face of the unsuspecting matron.

The shock of this didn't register for a second, but then Miss Crewell erupted. She hit Doris, pushed her up against a cubicle, and, not having a strap at hand, proceeded to slap her as best she could. When her initial rage abated she glared at Doris with cold anger.

"Your visiting privileges are suspended for one visit!" she snapped.

At that Doris didn't hesitate but took the mop and gave the matron another one in the face. It was a real good one this time, right in the mouth.

"Two visits!" Miss Crewell yelled, her arms flailing in fury as she spat out a mouthful of grimy floorwash.

That meant Doris wouldn't see her parents for over a month. The thought horrified me, but deep down inside I cheered for her.

Someone went to her parents on visiting day and explained why she wasn't there.

At times like that, parents were grateful to know that at the least their child wasn't sick. But it would be a couple more weeks before they'd be able to see their child for themselves. They'd have no idea how badly beaten the child was, or if there were bruises, or chunks of hair missing. The visit would be a long and lonely one. Some parents left immediately on learning their child wasn't able to see them. Others would huddle in with other parents, and try to learn more about why their child wasn't there, share the food they'd brought, shed some tears, and then kiss the child through the chain link fence and forward a message to their own child.

After the incident a bunch of us gathered round Doris and told her how brave she was. I too thought she was brave, but that sort of head-on confrontation with the matrons frightened me. They always had the upper hand, and we could never hope to beat them. It seemed to me that the best we could hope for in our situation was not to antagonize them, and to pray for strength to endure the rest.

* * *

Every time the health nurse came to the school, I shuddered. My pulse started pounding as soon as I saw her walk past the window. I always knew it was her because of her nurse's hat. I'd get almost physically ill at the sight of it.

When she walked into the room I tried to melt into my desk. I always hoped somehow she'd miss my name and I wouldn't get the big needle. I used to pray that just once she'd smile and reassure me it wouldn't hurt, but that never happened.

Afterwards I always kept my tears to myself, because if I were seen crying it would only make matters worse. First, I could expect a reprimand from the nurse, and then, when I got back to the dorm, another one from the matron. It didn't matter if we were at school or at play, we had to be always on the alert to avoid getting into any sort of situation which might require an explanation. There were so many ways we could unwittingly get into trouble that it was impossible to anticipate them all.

In May 1958 we all got special permission to go into downtown New Denver to watch the New Denver Centennial Celebrations. The big excitement was that our parents were allowed to join us. I could hardly believe my ears. My heart was pounding in anticipation of the day's activities.

We woke to the sun shining on our little town, which set the tone for what turned out to be a magical day. We ran downtown as soon as we were allowed, to meet up with our parents. Together we watched the parade celebrating the town's heritage, from the gold rush on. We watched donkey ball, cheering at the top of our lungs, and felt like normal children. Mom bought cotton candy for my sisters and me. As I was eating it I experienced such a feeling of joy and freedom that to this day I can still taste it. I was in a daze. I had only ever imagined life could be like this.

We had to report back to the dorm for a head count at lunchtime, but didn't have to eat there. We ran to the dorm, checked in to show we hadn't taken off for home with our families, and ran all the way back to town. My mom had prepared enough food for an army, and I ate until I thought I'd burst. What a feast! Every mouthful was exquisite, and the best thing was that we had all day to enjoy it.

We had such a beautiful visit. Many families picnicked together, and we shared love and laughter. But all too soon it was over, and we headed back to the dorm. I walked back slowly, dragging my feet, hoping that some day all my days could be like that one.

Deep down in my heart I knew that wouldn't be for a long, long time. A feeling of hopelessness came over me, and by the time I got back to the dorm I had resigned myself to it. The tears fell quickly and quietly as I sat on the floor under the window. The whole joyful day had become a painful reminder of how good life could be if we were only allowed to do the things other children took for granted.

18. DANCING TO ELVIS

Summer, 1958

There was some interest in our plight among the general public, and so during my years in New Denver the dorm saw a steady stream of journalists and reporters. Whenever members of the news media were coming there'd be a huge effort to have everything spotless. Matron bounced her dime on our blankets with true zeal. She ordered us to comb our hair again, or to change our clothing if she thought we weren't spruced up enough for the reporters. Every little corner was checked for dust. Even the books in the playroom were straightened on their shelves. We liked it when the media came, because the food was always better and the matrons seemed to be that little bit nicer.

Huge lightning storms were the norm during the summer. When the thunder clapped, a girl named Polly was beyond terrified. She'd jump under her bed and scream like crazy, crying and hollering about how scared she was. Matron would appear from the comfort of the office and yank Polly out from under the bed by her hair, threatening discipline and yelling at her not to be such a baby.

One day media were there when a storm rose. An enormous clap of thunder boomed overhead, at which Polly screamed and dived under the bed. Well, wouldn't you know, Matron lovingly bent down and spoke softly to Polly, telling her everything was all right and not to be afraid. Then, to our amazement, she sat on the bed and placed Polly on her lap while she pretended to kiss Polly's fears away. That photo appeared in either the Vancouver Sun or the Province newspaper.

The next storm? Polly got hauled out by her hair and was yelled at to grow up.

That summer Connie and I moved into the cubicles, which was the name given to the sleeping quarters for intermediate girls. It was a sign I was growing up, but it was also a painful reminder of how my childhood was steadily passing me by.

To get to the cubicles you went through the front door of the main building, into the girls' side of the dining room. To the left was the seating for the boys, and in between was the kitchen. To the right were the girls' cubicles. Each cubicle had six or eight beds and there were three of them, merely formed by placing dividing walls into what before had been one large dormitory room. A view of the lake made up one of the walls, and where a fourth wall should have been was open to the corridor. Across the way the bathrooms and the matron's office looked back towards the annex. The bathroom had a huge shower stall, a row of five or six sinks, and the toilets. Beyond the third cubicle was a short ramped hallway, and then a wide open room with twelve or fourteen beds in it, and an emergency exit at the far end. That was where the oldest girls slept.

I was moved into cubicle three and given a bed beside the window, from where I could look out at night and see the lake. *All the better for planning a getaway,* I reflected. Connie was put in cubicle two, and our beds were head-to-head with just the dividing wall between. There was a radiator against the wall, which allowed a little space for our hands to reach through. We could pass things to each other through the gap at night when we were supposed to be sleeping.

The shower stall was as big as a room, and there were lots of shower heads in it. There were a lot of toilets too. There were no doors on the toilets, but I was used to that, so it didn't bother me. The sinks were vast. I could probably have had a bath in one of them. The showers in the annex had been smaller, but these were huge. We were given no more time though, and we'd crowd in there, hoping that the five minutes we were allotted would be enough to get the soap out of our eyes and hair.

One good thing about being in the cubicles was that we didn't have to go outside to get to the dining room. Against that, living in the cubicles brought with it kitchen duties. Prior to mealtimes some of us had to help prepare the food. Our job would be to peel potatoes, carrots, and other vegetables, though sometimes we'd also prepare the salad, or set tables. The dishes were now our job too. After dinner there was no end of plates that needed washing, drying and putting away, and it took hours to do them.

Some of the older girls in the cubicles were quite mean to the younger children. I don't think they really wanted to be mean, but I guess it was safer for them to take out their anger on the smaller girls than on the matrons.

The matrons in the cubicles were mean too, just like in the annex, but they weren't as mean as the Hisser.

* * *

Although we were never allowed to go home to our families for holidays, the dorm did take us all on a holiday of our own one year. I don't know what prompted the director to do that. I guess he just decided we should go somewhere in the summer. We all wanted to go home of course, but that wasn't an option.

There were to be two groups. Group one, made up of the older children and accompanied by Mr. and Mrs. Stickler, was to go to Vancouver, and group two, made up of the children still in the annex, to Banff in the Rockies. Since I'd only been in the cubicles a short time and many of my friends were still in the annex, I wanted to go to Banff. Instead I was put in group one. I was very upset, and asked to be allowed to go with group two, but was denied. I was happy though to learn that Ruby and Irene were going to be in my group.

The truth is I really didn't want to go anywhere because of my tendency to throw up on long trips. I'd much rather have just stayed in New Denver by myself, but that idea too was quashed. I was told to quit complaining, to consider the trip an honour and a privilege, and not to forget to pack my bathing suit and toothpaste.

There was a certain element of suspense and anticipation before we left, as with any trip. I kind of liked the idea that I was going to Vancouver, because if the ship were coming up river on the way to New Denver I'd be able to see it. Then I could just get off the bus and jump aboard so I wouldn't miss going to Russia with my parents. Or maybe I'd jump off the bus in Grand Forks and hide out at Auntie Vatkin's. I was pretty sure she wouldn't sell her store to go to Russia.

These were all great ideas, but the moment I stepped on the bus the smell of diesel fumes hit my stomach, and I was gagging before I even found my seat.

The road out of New Denver was so narrow that as we went past the Cape a car coming towards us had to back up because there wasn't enough room to pass. I looked out the window and my heart turned flip flops when I saw the huge drop-off towards the lake. I prayed the driver of the bus knew what he was doing.

I think I travelled about two miles before I started throwing up. I missed most of the scenery on the way to Vancouver through either throwing up or lying on the seat with my jacket over my head. I was so sick I wished I was dead. I guess no one believed me when I'd told them I got travel sick. The only consolation would have been if I could have thrown up on Mr. Stickler, but he was too far away. We stopped in Penticton for the night. I had a nice time when I wasn't throwing up.

The next day we continued on to Vancouver. We stayed at the Hastings Community Centre there, sleeping on the floor in sleeping bags. Across the street was the Playland Amusement Park. We never got to go, which was just as well, as I'd known I was afraid of heights ever since Auntie Vatkin took me on the ferris wheel in Grand Forks many years earlier. I'd protested, but my auntie wouldn't hear of my not going up with her. She dragged me over and plunked me in the seat, then cuddled in beside me. The ferris wheel was set up overlooking the edge of a slope, and as we were coming down I was certain death was seconds away. The more I cried in fear the harder my aunt held me, and the harder she laughed. She was my teacher extraordinaire in many aspects of life, but helping me overcome my fear of heights wasn't one of them.

As we looked at the Playland roller coaster hurtling its dazzling way through the night sky, our fertile minds went to work. I pictured myself hanging on for dear life as the ride got wilder and wilder, screaming for help and enjoying the thrill of the ups and downs. I've always believed it's a good thing we have our imagination. That way we can enjoy the things we'd never want to do in real life.

While in Vancouver we went to Grouse Mountain, which even in July still had a small cap of snow on the peak. I thought we were going to look at the mountain and then go back to the Centre, but no; the chair lift was operating, and we were given the opportunity to take a ride to the top and then down again.

I couldn't believe it. "They want us to go on that thing?!"

A row of flimsy chairs hung from a thin cable by an even flimsier metal hook. The cable stretched between pylons clinging precariously to the jagged mountainside and then disappeared into a shimmering haze way, way up high. Eagles, and quite possibly other birds of prey, circled overhead.

"Um... I'd rather stay down here, if it's all right with... yaaaarghh!" I screamed as I was suddenly lifted bodily from behind. "No! Don't make me!" I panicked. "I don't want to go!"

"It'll be fun. You'll see."

"No, it won't! It won't! Please, leave me down here! I won't run away, I promise!"

I put up quite a struggle. Not a mop-in-the face struggle, but a struggle nonetheless. But the adults grabbed me and pushed me onto the slowly-moving chair, then quickly closed the bar.

Oh Lord, I thought. *I'm on the chair lift! I'm going to die!*

My worst nightmare had come true. I was heading for the top of the mountain, my feet dangling over empty space, trying not to look at the trees and rocks far below, and sitting beside me was Mrs. Stickler. We appeared to be moving at breakneck speed, and the chair was swinging wildly. My heart was in my throat, and I was crying.

"Can we go back?" I sobbed. "Is it too late to go back?"

"There, there!" Mrs. Stickler tried to comfort me, but without success.

"But we have to go back anyway," I argued. "Can't we just go back now?"

"Do stop fussing, child!"

All the way up the mountain my anxiety doubled, knowing we'd have do it all over again coming back down. At the top a photographer was waiting for us as we came in to land.

"Smile, now!" Mrs. Stickler ordered.

Smiling was the last thing I felt like doing, but I was afraid of discipline later, so I obeyed her.

Quick! Quick! Take the darn picture now before I throw up, I thought, smiling through teeth clenched against the rising in my gullet. I still have the photo. It shows what appears to be a mother and daughter on an outing, having a good time.

I didn't enjoy Grouse Mountain. We did a tour of Vancouver, and then headed back to New Denver. On the way we stopped in Penticton again, where we were allowed to go for a swim in Okanagan Lake. The water there is shallow quite a long way out. Irene and I waded out into water that only came up to our waists, but because it was so far out into the lake it looked from the beach as if it had to be very deep. We decided to show off by pretending we were doing the front crawl, the butterfly stroke, and other strange inventions of our own, while in fact our feet were still on the bottom. We had a great time performing for the kids on the beach, who thought we were doing our fancy acrobatics in very deep water.

The trip was uneventful but for the throwing up and the fear of heights, and the ever-present anxiety to please our caregivers. As we drove into New Denver and passed people working in their yards, playing with their children, mowing the lawn, just doing regular stuff, my heart ached for home. I was actually glad to be back at the dorm, where the ground was solid and familiar and I didn't have to get into a vehicle. I never thought I'd ever make a statement like that. However, the truth being what it is, I was glad to be back at what I now realized had become my second home.

I really prayed too that for the remainder of my days in New Denver we wouldn't be offered another holiday. My prayer was answered, and I was pleased, because I had no desire to puke my way through any more trips.

After we got back we had to write an essay about the trip. I guess maybe the media were going to be shown how good life was at the dorm. We were told what to write, but Alex, Eugene and Polly wrote the truth. They were punished with no swimming or playing for the whole summer; instead they were given extra chores. Alex had to wash windows, of which there were plenty at the dorm. He and Eugene were made to stay on the sunny side while doing the windows, instead of being allowed to work in the shade. He also had to rake the beach, and help in the laundry, working alongside people who got paid. He was even made to babysit Stickler's young son William. He didn't like to do it, because God help him if something should happen while he was in charge.

Alex was also made to carry Stickler's clubs from the dorm to the golf course. They were heavy, and it was quite a distance away. Stickler would tell him to start walking around eleven o'clock, and Alex knew he'd miss lunch. Then Stickler would drive by and wait for Alex to show up at the course. Stickler would stay late, chat and eat, while Alex was made to wait for him to finish up. It was the same on the way home; Stickler would drive by while Alex struggled to carry the clubs. By the time Alex got back to the dorm, dinner was finished. Too bad, because now he had to wait for breakfast. Alex was hungry all the time.

Sometimes on the way home a bunch of the town boys would wait for Alex beside an apple tree. They'd pepper him with the apples, and he'd have bruises for the next couple of days. Sometimes he'd eat a couple of the apples even if they were green because he knew there'd be no dinner when he got back to the dorm.

Stickler sometimes played golf two or three times a week.

* * *

That summer the newspapers reported that the government of the Soviet Union had decided to accept the application by Sons of Freedom Doukhobors to re-migrate to Russia. It was also reported that the Canadian federal government and the British Columbia provincial government had agreed to help with the move. It looked as if the proposed relocation of Freedomites to Russia was finally going to happen. My father was happy; after all, it meant his trip had been a success. But the prospect left me even more apprehensive than ever. In fact, it filled me with dread.

* * *

One of the older girls had a record player, and sometimes we younger girls were allowed to listen to the records the older girls had. One visiting day my auntie gave me an amazing gift. She knew some of the older folks wouldn't like the idea, so she passed it to me over the fence wrapped in a paper bag. It was a long-playing record by Elvis Presley called Elvis' Golden Records. It had all his best songs, from 'Heartbreak Hotel', his first big hit, to songs such as 'Jailhouse Rock' and 'Love Me Tender'. I was ecstatic! I knew it was a gift I'd treasure forever. When they found out about it, some of the children said I'd burn in hell just for having it. Others listened to it with dreamy eyes while Elvis crooned and jumped. I even let the older girls keep it overnight sometimes. I wrote the number eighty-five on the cover so everyone would know it belonged to me. I only hoped we wouldn't wear it out, because we listened to it all the time.

One Saturday night we watched a movie about Calamity Jane. It was a musical set in the Wild West, with Doris Day singing and dancing in the lead role, and it inspired Anna and Natalie and me to try our hand at acting. We borrowed some fancy clothes from the other girls, and managed to borrow the record player too. We collected what we could as stage props, then set up on the girls' verandah and danced in crazy outfits to Elvis and Ricky Nelson. Our costumes were borrowed crinolines, jewelry, fancy skirts, anything we could get our hands on. We danced till we thought our legs would fall off. Our friends thought we were very brave. Lots of children gathered at the bottom of the steps to watch us. They cheered us on as we danced the cancan and made up a variety of our own dances. It was thrilling to hear the sound of their applause. The boys made fun of us, but we didn't care. We were having fun in our own little world. The dancing was such an escape that for a while it almost helped me forget where I was. I was teased a lot and called Calamity Jane for a long time.

We were so well received that we started to perform on a regular basis. One of the reasons I enjoyed it was that I remembered the girls in the blue crepe-paper dresses from our school concert. I wanted to dress up pretty and glide around on the stage. Dancing on the dormitory verandah was almost as good as that concert, except that this time our clothes were real and not made of paper.

The matrons encouraged us to carry on, but some of the children told us we were doing the work of the devil.

"It's true!" they'd say. "If you do that, the devil will possess you, and you'll be assimilated into the ways of the matrons!"

I knew it wasn't true, because I knew who I was and nobody was going to scare me from doing something I really enjoyed.

My grandfather wasn't as forthright, but he certainly had his opinion on dancing. The Zebroffs were very religious, God-fearing people, and dancing was not to be condoned, under any circumstances. I didn't want to disappoint them, so I never told them about any of the things I wasn't supposed to do. I did try to please my grandfather though, in that I never went to sleep without first saying the prayers he and Grandma had taught me. I also sang the songs I'd learned from them. I believed that we should have fun, pray, and not get so involved in one thing that we lose sight of all that there is.

Deep down I'd always been a happy child, eager for new adventures and things to do. The experience of New Denver introverted me, making me afraid of everything. But when on occasion my spirit surged forth, nothing could stop me.

Some of the children in residence criticized me for wanting to sing and dance and live life to the full. Other children encouraged me to be true to myself, and not pay attention to what anyone else was saying. My inner self said it was okay, and I tried hard to listen to that voice.

My auntie had given me a camera, a small Kodak Brownie, and it was one of my most prized possessions. When we weren't dancing on the verandah, I loved to get Anna and Natalie and some of the other children to pose for me. I'd sit them on the verandah steps with a guitar and tell them to pretend they were models or pop stars. I'd pose them this way and that until they yelled at me in frustration. I'd ignore them, and just carry on giving directions. Some of the poses required them to lean over backwards so far they could hardly straighten out afterwards. I'd pass the exposed roll to my parents through the fence. I'm sure my Auntie paid for the developing because my parents wouldn't usually have had the money to do it themselves.

19. RAGE AT THE WORLD

Fall, 1958 – Spring, 1959

As summer came to an end and the fall weather moved down the mountain it became too cold to dance in the open air. Besides, by now Anna and Natalie and I felt we'd taken our play-acting on the verandah about as far as it could go, and were ready to take the next step to stardom.

"And what's that?"

"We put on a show indoors."

"In the playroom?"

"No. In the gym!"

"We'd need to ask for permission first."

"And Matron would never agree to it."

Anna shrugged. "It can't hurt to ask."

"What sort of a show?" Matron asked.

The question took us by surprise. We hadn't really thought that far ahead.

"Um... singing...?"

"...dancing...?"

"...maybe even a little play for the kids...?"

She furrowed her brow to give the impression of deep thought. "Let me think about it. I'll let you know."

To our surprise, permission was granted. "You can have the use of the gym this coming Saturday evening," Matron told us.

Anna and I could hardly believe our good fortune, but Natalie was worried. She pointed out that as we'd presumed we'd be denied, we hadn't anything prepared at all.

"She's right. We don't actually have a show to put on."

"And Saturday's just two days away."

"Hmmm... That's true. We need an idea."

We pondered collectively.

"It's got to be good."

"It's got to be colourful."

"And it's replacing the movie. So it's got to be better than anything Hollywood can offer."

Anna was the first to speak. "No problem. We'll just wing it!"

"What!"

"You mean..."

"No script, no rehearsal. Just do it!"

I wasn't convinced. "That's your best idea?"

Neither was Natalie. "Are you even allowed to do that?"

But Anna was already dizzy with her own enthusiasm. "But of course! It'll be so much better that way. So spontaneous! So raw! So authentic!"

"I'm really nervous..."

"But that's good! That's what gives you the actor's edge!"

"But..."

"Come on, girls!" Anna put her hands on her hips, the way the matrons did when they thought we were being more than usually difficult. "Is this really the three musketeers I'm hearing? All for one, one for all, and game for anything?"

Natalie and I were silent for a moment. "All right. But we'll need to agree in advance what it is we're winging about."

Anna smiled. "Trust me!"

"If this is going to be a proper performance - you know, with seats and everything - shouldn't we be charging admission?" Natalie asked.

"I don't have a good feeling about asking for money," I said. "We don't even..."

"No, she's right. We shouldn't be doing this for nothing. And besides, these plays might go on for a long time. We'll need money so we can buy stuff to make costumes with."

"Plays?" It had never occurred to me there might be more than just the one. But Anna and Natalie were already way ahead of me.

"And also jewelry..."

"...that, of course, we can wear outside of performances."

Once again we had to get permission from Matron, who again did her furrowing thing.

"As long as it's not more than a nickel," she said finally.

I could hardly believe it. Not only were we allowed to do something we loved, but we were to be paid for it as well!

"Only a nickel?" whined Natalie. "Doesn't she know how much jewelry costs these days?"

"A nickel seems fair," said Anna. "Especially since we don't even have a show yet."

The next couple of days were a flurry of activity.

"Have you heard?" Natalie was delirious with excitement. "Everyone I've spoken to is planning to come to our play!"

"I know," Anna said. "Some of them are even borrowing money so they can attend."

I was worried. "If their parents ask what it's for we could be in big trouble."

"Why?"

"It's bad enough some of the kids think this is the work of the devil," I said, "but I sure wouldn't want to be cursed by some of those old-timers."

"Some of them are pretty scary," Natalie agreed.

"True, but we don't have time to think about curses and stuff," Anna said. "There's a play to put on!"

* * *

The older boys finished setting out the chairs, and the audience was thronging into the gymnasium. Almost every child in residence was there. The money was collected by Anna's elder sister Nayda; as the container filled with nickels, so did our heads with visions of fame and stardom. We had an announcer. I peeked out from behind the door as she welcomed the crowd. Our hearts were pounding, because our plan for the evening was to taunt some of the more prominent boys in the dorm, particularly the ones we had a secret crush on. We still hadn't worked out exactly how it would happen, but were keeping our fingers crossed that everything would turn out well.

Alex and Eugene, two of the boys we planned to torment, picked front row seats as we knew they would, and the performance began. We picked on one, and then the other. We'd sing a song, do a little dance, mimic a movie we'd seen recently, and then start all over again. The crowd loved us. The boys we were taunting could do little more than clench their fists at us and make obscene gestures. We knew we'd get it from them later, but this was our moment and we just kept going. We also knew that deep down the boys were enjoying it. After all, how often did they get to be the subject of an evening's entertainment?

We were a smash hit. The children loved us, and asked us to perform again. We only did one more concert though. We took in a grand total of five dollars from the first one, and had plans to buy crepe paper and other assorted goods to make costumes with for the next one, but the girl we entrusted the money to had other plans, and we never did see any of it. So our fame was short-lived, but we enjoyed it while it lasted. We were children after all, and the attention span of most of us was pretty short. Hollywood won out in the end, as I guess we all knew it had to.

Theatre took our minds off the situation we were in. It allowed us to scream and yell, which wasn't allowed under normal circumstances. It felt wonderful to rage at the world and pretend it was part of the play. We also knew that as long as we kept entertaining, the matrons softened toward us somewhat, and even pretended to take an interest in what we were doing.

Photography afforded me much the same liberty. As long as I was running around with my camera, rounding up children for photos, the smiles were always in evidence. Once more I'd found a way to enjoy myself with the approval of the matrons. It seemed to me we were always being watched, and we were. But as long as we appeared to be busy we were left alone. I learned this fact soon after arriving in New Denver, and found all sorts of ways to appear to be doing one thing when in actual fact I was up to something else. We were only young, but we learned early on how to play the game, and excelled in a very short time.

* * *

That winter we heard the police had approached the green lady about the food she was storing for us. I guess the director must have heard she was hiding food for us, and decided to put a stop to it.

When the police turned up they asked if they could look in her root cellar.

"Do you have a search warrant?"

"There's no need to worry, ma'am. This is just an informal request."

"Am I under arrest?"

"Good Lord, no! Ha! ha! We just want..."

"Then get the hell off my property!"

That's the way we heard it. They said they wanted to look in her root cellar and she told them to go to hell. And they did. At least, they left her property without looking in the cellar. If any of us ever dared speak to a matron like that they'd have had to scrape what was left of us off the walls. We talked about it for weeks afterwards. As we did, the suspicion began to dawn that even the police with their guns and dogs and clubs were more open to reason than our caregivers.

The green lady was my heroine after that. I wanted to be brave like her, but I also knew I'd have to be really grown up before I could talk like she did and get away with it. In the meantime, whenever a matron yelled at me I could now look her straight in the eye and say "Yes, Matron," but in my head I'd be saying, '...and get the hell off my property!"

One day we had a spelling test. Connie and I tied for first place, so we both won a prize. Since my surname came earlier in the alphabet, our teacher Mrs. Kelly said I could choose my prize before Connie.

"Don't pick the necklace," Connie whispered as I went up to the front.

The necklace Connie had so set her heart on was very beautiful. I'd never owned anything like it. I didn't wear any sort of jewelry at home, partly because we were poor and partly because my family was so religious. I wanted it badly, so I picked it.

Connie was heartbroken. "It's not fair," she said. "After all, it was mine, really! I did as well on the test as you!"

She was so mad at me she wouldn't be my friend for a couple of days. I loved her dearly, but not enough to give up the necklace.

I told Jimmy about that, and about other arguments I had with girls, and listened carefully in case he had the answers for me. I cried myself to sleep holding him close, knowing he was the only one there I trusted to care for me. I told him my hopes for what I wanted to be when I grew up: a stewardess, or a lawyer, maybe even a bullfighter. I shared my prayers with him, giving thanks to the Lord that I was okay, and surviving the hell hole I was in. Most of all I shared with him my desire to go home, and be a part of a normal, regular family.

The older girls from the dormitory also liked my Jimmy. I let them hold him too sometimes. I'd heard that some of them had got their period. I hadn't yet, but I knew that when you got your period you could have a baby. I guessed that was why the older girls liked to hold Jimmy, because he felt like a real baby. I hoped none of the girls would ever have a baby there. I sure wouldn't want my child to grow up in prison.

I heard that when you get your period it hurts, and it's really messy. I didn't want to get my period when I was still in the cubicles. I wouldn't tell anyone even if I did. All the girls would be watching to see what I'd do. And it wouldn't be just the girls, either. The boys always asked who got it.

* * *

It was during my stay in New Denver that I fell in love for the very first time. His name was Eugene, and a handsomer man you couldn't hope to find anywhere. All the girls loved Eugene; the young girls as much as the older girls. I don't remember too much about Eugene in my early years, except that he combed his hair an awful lot. But by the time I was eleven he was the boy of my dreams. He'd look at me and smile, and I'd be in heaven. I was sure I'd marry him someday, we'd have babies, and we'd live happily ever after. I was even convinced he felt the same.

Then he proved it.

For Valentine's Day that year I bought a book of cards with valentine sayings on them for my classmates, and cut them out. It was a big book, and it took a long time to get every little card out. On the day itself, as usual, we each had a big brown envelope taped to the side of our desk. Some envelopes were pretty much full. Mine was about half full. I could hardly wait to read the cards in it.

One was in a large envelope, and said 'To My Sweetheart' on the front. I could tell it was no ordinary card, and wondered who could have given it to me. I was excited to open it, but also a little apprehensive, because I didn't want to be a sweetheart to just anyone. Part of me also thought maybe it was all a mistake, and I'd have to give the card to the proper person.

I couldn't imagine it coming from anyone other than Alex. But, to my surprise, it was from Eugene. There it was, signed for all the world to see, 'Love, Eugene'. Alex gave me a nice card too, but it was like the ones I gave out, not a store-bought, special one.

I could hardly breathe.

So he really did love me, after all!

Well, my overactive eleven-year-old imagination went to work right away. It was true; we would marry! I could start naming the babies at recess. As I was on my way back to the dorm for lunch break I was so happy I felt I was walking on air. My heart was singing, my feet were dancing. I wanted to shout 'Hooray!'

Lena came running towards me. In her hand she clutched a bundle of envelopes, including a large one about the size of mine. She was very excited, but before she could say anything I pulled out Eugene's card.

"Lena! Look what I got!"

"Never mind that - look what I got!"

She shoved a card into my hand with a very smug look on her face.

"That's strange," I said. "It's just like mine."

I was curious to see who'd sent my card to Lena. When I opened it, my whole world collapsed.

Inside were the words, 'Love, Eugene'.

I was in shock.

Eugene had sent Lena a card identical to mine!

We compared the cards, the handwriting inside. The evidence was clear.

"Seems our Eugene is a two-timer," Lena concluded grimly, "and we haven't even gone on a date with him yet!"

We weren't allowed to date at the dorms, as we wouldn't be even at home. Nevertheless we liked to pretend that if we were at home we'd be allowed to do things forbidden us in New Denver. In reality, our parents held us to very strict standards of behaviour.

"I guess he wanted to cover all the bases," I said to Lena later as we lay on our backs in the fort.

"Who are you talking about?"

"Who do you think?" I said. "The Romeo of New Denver!"

"If by that you mean Eugene, he can cover my bases anytime!"

We sniggered, not quite sure what it meant, but knowing the older girls talked like that all the time.

"I guess he wanted us both to feel special," I said, trying to mask the hurt I still felt.

"Maybe we did. At least, for a moment or two."

"I wonder how many cards he actually gave out."

"You mean maybe he wanted to cover more bases than just ours?"

"Lena, you're awful!"

"I know!" I said, an idea coming to me. "Let's not tell him, ever!"

"Why would we want to do that?"

"Just let him believe he pulled a fast one on us!"

"Okay, but why?"

"So he'll always be wondering if one of us will find out. And then come and scratch his eyes out!"

"Let him sweat it out, you mean?"

"Yeah! Something like that."

"Helen?"

"What?"

"Don't you think maybe you're taking this all a bit too seriously?"

I pondered for a while in silence.

"Lena?"

"What?"

"Do you think maybe Eugene really meant what he said on my card, and only sent one to you out of pity?"

* * *

The last time my eyes were checked was in grade four. By this time the chalkboard was a blur. If I wanted to copy from it I had to be just inches away. Most of the time though, I tried to remember what the teacher said and worked from that, instead of from the board. I asked repeatedly for glasses, but was denied each time. I spent my last year in New Denver squinting at everyone and everything.

One visiting day in late spring, as always, I searched out my parents' face in the crowd while we sang the usual hymns. But when I found them, I could tell at once that something was different. My mother seemed more radiant that day, my father a little more careful for her well-being. When we finished singing, my sisters raced to our usual meeting spot by the fence, jumping up and down impatiently at my approach, only too eager to blurt out the news that soon there would be an addition to the family.

The news caught me off guard. I responded cheerfully, and joined in the general excitement, but as soon as I could I escaped to the fort, flung myself on the ground, and wept my heart out. I should have been happy at the news, and no doubt a part of me was, on some level. But deep down inside I felt only an empty, aching sense of loss.

My family was changing, and I was no longer a part of it.

20. FINAL SUMMER

Summer, 1959

I'd always believed in God as the Creator of life, of the universe, of all that there is. As my time in New Denver went on, this belief grew, but also developed into a very personal conviction.

One night I was lying awake in cubicle three. The air had been warm and sticky for days, and I was unable to get to sleep. Suddenly, out of nowhere, a hush descended on the world that was so quiet it made the hairs on the back of my neck stand on end. I looked out the window, wondering what was going on. I could see nothing unusual, but couldn't shake a sense of profound unease.

As I watched, the sky over the lake turned dark. Ominous clouds piled in from behind the mountains, and fat drops of rain began to plop into the mirror-like sheen on the surface of the lake. Trees along the shore, which had been motionless, suddenly began to whip back and forth as if they were being picked up and shaken by a giant hand. Within minutes thunder rumbled and lightning crashed overhead. Rain pounded the roof and rattled against the windows. Clouds raced, broke up, regrouped and were torn to shreds again. I'd experienced many summer storms during my time in New Denver but this one dwarfed them all with its beauty and destructive power. Awed, I leaned against the window and watched the terror and magnificence unfolding outside.

Struck by how small and helpless we are against the unrestrained forces of nature, I found myself thinking about death. I recall contemplating the finality of it: once you're gone, you're gone. For the next few weeks the thought haunted me. I'd lie awake, frightened, reflecting over and over on the inescapable fact that no one could escape death, and that once it happened it was forever.

I didn't feel there was anyone I could talk to about this. It wasn't a subject you just jumped into. I continued to ponder the mystery of death on my own.

Then one night something inside me said, *what if that's not the case? What if there's life after death?*

Life after death? Remember, I was eleven years old. This was pretty heavy stuff.

Nevertheless, the idea gelled in my mind. I recall starting conversations involving the new word 'reincarnation'. Some of the children thought I was crazy, but a couple of them agreed with me. I was amazed and relieved. I hadn't suspected others might think the same way as I did.

From then on, although life in New Denver continued to be as harsh as ever, it was somewhat easier for me to bear. I came to believe that no matter how bad things were in the dorm, I'd endured worse in previous lifetimes. I began to look at my life as one huge lesson, with lots of fringe benefits. The experience of New Denver had been given to me as an opportunity to learn and grow in this lifetime, while the love, laughter and caring I shared with some of the children there were all bonuses.

The belief system I discovered in New Denver is still with me today. I was raised Christian, and always kept that part, but added to it. I became a spiritualist, without knowing what the word meant.

* * *

We still liked to retreat to our secret fort, where we could do the things girls everywhere have always done in spite of the opposition of the staff and the disapproval of our families. We'd talk about boys, why they were so immature, and what we wanted to do when we grew up. That was the summer when I was about to turn twelve, and elaborate fantasies of escaping the confines of my existence were tempered by fear of the still-unknown world of adulthood we'd inevitably have to face one day.

One of us had got hold of some makeup. This was top secret contraband, for we were still way too young, and knew that if we were caught using it we'd get in big trouble not just from the matrons but from our parents as well. We coloured our eyes, our cheeks and our lips, and then passed around a little mirror so we could admire ourselves. We looked like clowns, but in our minds we were all grown up and looking beautiful.

I reminded Irene of what she'd told me about her brother years before, when we were both in the annex. Now I was finally in the cubicles and summer was coming, I didn't want to miss the spectacle.

"What's that?" some of the others asked.

"You mean you haven't heard? Irene, tell them!"

Irene pursed her lips. "It's my brother, Eddie," she announced solemnly, as if admitting some dark, forbidden secret. "He has dreams that tell the future. And, because of old Indian connections - which I can't go into - he's able to walk on water!"

"No way!"

"He can walk on water?"

"That's the coolest thing I've heard all week!"

We were all suitably awed, as Irene no doubt intended.

"Can we see him do it?"

"Can he do it now?"

"It can only happen during a full moon in the middle of summer," Irene said, her voice dropping to a whisper. "*And he can only be seen by people who've been sworn to secrecy!*"

Irene had a way of speaking in italics that was thrilling. It was dramatic. Conspiratorial. It was the sort of thing the fort was built for.

All that summer we looked forward to seeing Eddie perform his moonlit stroll. Matron would do a walk through the cubicles, and as soon as she was out of sight we'd appoint a lookout. The rest of us would scramble to the windows overlooking the lake, hoping to behold the wondrous sight. None of us ever saw it happen, but we sure watched for him during each full moon.

The hardest part about the dorm was that there was no family life there at all. I missed the hugs and kisses I used to get at home, and I really missed the good food my mom and grandma used to cook for us. Our lives in New Denver were lived in a succession of big rooms, with no privacy, ever. I think most of us forgot what a regular home felt like.

Just outside the gate were three houses where some of the staff lived. When John Stickler was director he lived there with his wife, and his son and daughters. His house had a lush green lawn all the way around. We used to stand on our side of the fence and watch his daughters play in their yard. I remember the sounds of laughter that came from their property. I'd get upset because it reminded me of playing with my little sisters at home. We were never acknowledged, and certainly not invited to join in whatever game they were playing.

However, Brenda and Elaine were allowed to come into our playground. We had to be very careful when they were over. Children squabble. Well, if we wanted the swing and so did one of the girls, and we wouldn't give in, they'd run crying. And then whoever made them cry would be in big trouble.

In June of that year, my youngest sister Marie turned eight. After that I didn't see either of my sisters much. When they did come they were wary of all that was going on around them, and the visit would be strained.

* * *

One movie we saw around that time was 'The Searchers', with John Wayne and Natalie Wood. The character played by Natalie was kidnapped by the Indians, and John Wayne, who played her uncle in the movie, set out to find her. It took him years, and she was all grown up when he found her, and she didn't want to return to her family.

It reminded some of us of our situation. Most of us had grown accustomed to being in the dorm, and couldn't imagine life outside. We all desperately wanted to go home, but the more time passed, the more we came to accept that this was our real home. Maybe some of us even gave up hope of ever being reunited with our families. The dream, so long unfulfilled, had come to seem more like a mirage. The fact was that over the years, life in New Denver had assumed a familiarity that made it much easier to accept it as the one undeniable reality that shaped our lives.

We didn't go away on holiday that year. Instead, we spent the summer in and around the dorm.

Whenever we got the chance we'd play all kinds of outdoor games. One day a bunch of us decided to play 'kick the can.' We had the whole world to hide in, and no rules about how far we could go. That meant we weren't restricted to the dorm property, but could look for places to hide anywhere in the Japanese village, or even beyond. We'd learned how to jump over the chain link fence without ripping our clothing so as to avoid being spotted trying to sneak out the main gate. This was one of my favourite games, and I was good at it. Whoever had to do the looking would sometimes spend the whole day trying to get out of that position, and often failed.

We started playing right after breakfast, only broke off for mealtimes, and continued until it was time to go in for bed. I was exhausted, and started retching. Normally this would go unnoticed, but I was dry-heaving and sweating heavily. Matron called the doctor, who immediately put me in the hospital, where I stayed for two or three days. The official reason was that I had the flu, but I believe all the running and sweating dehydrated me.

It was a pleasure to be in the hospital. The food was excellent, and I enjoyed the company of some of the other patients there. I had no desire to go back to the dorm, and dreamed up all kinds of excuses to stay. They didn't work, and I was soon released to the stranglehold of the caregivers once again.

Sure seemed like a holiday to me.

We spent a lot of time on the beach that summer. Many of us got so dark that our families could hardly recognize us. We always made bets about who could get the darkest.

As in previous years, I enjoyed swimming. By now I was ready to go into the senior swim program, and I felt I'd really accomplished something. But sometimes I didn't feel there was much to be happy about. One evening a group of us were singing around the campfire. Many years later, watching an archival film of that moment, I saw myself and I couldn't help but cry. My lips were moving, but that was all. My eyes were darting, my shoulders were hunched. I looked like a caged animal, whose life force had all but been removed.

I looked like I'd given in.

21. FREE AT LAST
August, 1959

After six long years of protest our parents finally understood that the government was not going to change its stance, and that continued resistance was pointless. The men were reluctant to capitulate, but didn't stand in the way of allowing their womenfolk to act in what they felt to be the best interests of their families.

So on the last Friday of July, 1959, our parents all travelled up to the courthouse in Nelson. There they signed official papers and solemnly promised to send their children to school when the new term began in September. In return, the magistrate authorized the release of all children held in New Denver under the care of the Department of Child Welfare. Buses were organized for the following Sunday to drive us all to Krestova, where we'd be returned to our parents.

Our release was announced on the radio. There was a lot of yelling and commotion as the news spread, and then in an instant the frenzy turned to silence as the names of the children to be released began to be read out. I was tense beyond belief. Could it really be true? After so long away from our families, were we really going home at last? I strained to hear my name over the hushed, urgent tones growing around me.

"What's he saying?"

"What name was that?"

"Was that me? Did he just say my name?"

"Shut up! I can't hear!"

All went quiet again as the voice continued to crackle through the speaker, announcing name after name of children I'd come to know as friends. Each name read out was one more child who'd be returning home. Each name was one more friend I'd possibly never see again. I turned away.

"Don't you want to hear if you're on the list?"

"I can't stand here while he goes through seventy-odd names. I'd rather be packing."

Others, too, broke away.

"Aren't you worried you might not be on the list?"

'I'm getting on that bus, if I have to climb up the exhaust pipe!'

Two buses came for us on that first Sunday in August. We knew they were really coming when we saw the huge clouds of dust on the highway just after lunch. I was relieved to know I was truly going home at last. *Thank you, Lord!* I grabbed my case and ran outside to wait my turn to board.

We got on as our names were called. Nora and Simon, a sister and brother, stood waiting. Simon's development was a little delayed, and Nora was quite protective of him. Simon's name was called and he boarded. Nora held her breath, waiting impatiently for her name to be called as the buses rapidly filled with children. My name was called. I rushed forward and took my seat, pinching myself to make sure it was really happening. I could see Nora getting more and more desperate as the buses filled up.

"What about me?" she kept saying. "I want to sit with my brother!"

Outside, the last names were announced from the list on matron's clipboard. The last children scrambled aboard as the great engines started up.

"That's it," Matron said. "That's everyone!"

"Wait!" cried Nora . "My name's not been called!"

One of the other matrons took Nora by the hand and tried to lead her away.

"Let me go!" Nora cried, "I have to be with my brother!"

She put up a struggle, but to no avail. The caregiver was much bigger and stronger, and Nora was dragged away.

Nora started screaming. She had no idea why she'd been separated from her brother and none of the caregivers was trying to comfort her or even explain it to her. She was still yelling and screaming as the buses pulled out.

That was our final sight and sound of the dormitory.

We were past Silverton when I reached in my case for my precious Jimmy, to comfort me. Panic set in when I couldn't find him. I racked my memory, and finally realized I'd left him sitting on my bed in his usual spot. I cried, and asked the driver to go back for him, but he told me that was impossible.

I later wrote to New Denver and pleaded for his return, but my letter was never answered.

My parents met the bus in Krestova, and drove me home. A photo of me with my mother and sisters appeared on the front page of the Grand Forks Gazette that week, announcing my return. In the picture my mother is seven months pregnant.

It was extremely hard to fit into the family on my return. My sisters and I had been very close before New Denver, but now there was a different pecking order. Kathrine had become the older sister in my absence, and didn't want to give up that role, especially with a new baby on the way. My sisters were naturally happy I was home, but they resented the fact that I was now heard more than they were. By that I mean my parents paid a little more attention to me now that I was around twenty-four hours a day. Of course, everyone wanted to know all about New Denver, and I was only too glad to oblige. I was also a smart mouth, having learned to stand on my own for the past three years and eight months. So, I guess for a short time I was forgiven for my attitude, which was to challenge everyone and everything.

But at the same time I found it hard to accept I was truly free. I'd watch in amazement as my younger sisters helped themselves to food when it wasn't lunch or supper time. They'd argue about bedtime, and then get to stay up later. My sisters tried to get to the food first, because they remembered how I always got the nicest food brought to me in New Denver, and at this point they were not overly happy to share.

Through learning to survive in a very strict environment I'd become used to being totally organized in everything I did. When my sisters, or even one of my parents, dropped something, a towel, or a piece of clothing, I'd be on them like a matron. My parents told me not to be bossy, but in my mind I was still in New Denver, and I knew what could happen for disobeying rules. Once my dad sat on the chesterfield and got the cover all messed up. When he rose to go and do something I jumped up and fixed the cover. Well, on my Dad's return he yanked the cover, setting it deliberately askew, then looked me in the eye and said defiantly that ours was a home, and not a house.

I was torn between wanting to make my parents and my sisters happy, and thinking they were all slobs.

I developed opinions on everything. At the ripe old age of twelve I'd argue with anyone about anything, because I'd had to think for myself all those years just to avoid punishment. I was self-reliant, but I was a mess. In hindsight, I'm certain a visit to a psychiatrist would have been in order. I'd learned how not to show emotion, and now that I was back with my gentle, loving mother again I'd forgotten how to be a good daughter. My mom was always patient with me, but I'm sure she thought I was a child from hell. I wanted our house to run as smoothly as New Denver did. Organized, meals on time, a set time for play. I was like a sergeant major; bossy, bossy, bossy.

My dad was not overly affectionate at any time, and I think that's why we got along fairly well. He wasn't much for hugs and kisses, and I was okay with that because it had been missing all those years anyway. It felt foreign to have Mom hug me for no reason at all. I'd accepted her affection while behind the fence, but then it was only for an hour and now it was surrounding me all the time. I'd almost lost any sense of compassion I'd gained, for when one of my sisters got ill, it was just another day and I knew they'd get over it, just as I used to while away. I'd become cold, and seemingly uncaring, but deep down inside I just wanted to be loved. It took a long time to accept that I was home to stay, and that my parents weren't going to let me be taken away again. I had a serious anxiety about being abandoned, and to this day I still fear being left alone with only myself to carry on.

After my release, my mother took me to an optometrist in the United States and I finally got the glasses I needed. A whole new world opened up for me. I was so happy to be able to follow in school and to read in comfort again. Even so, much as I liked going to the public school in Grand Forks, with my newfound freedom I'd feign illness, knowing my mother would believe me. Then I'd spend the day at home reading, playing by myself, or just lying around doing nothing. My father gave me credit for being smarter than I was, and told my sisters to listen to me because I was older. This caused huge resentment among us. We worked everything out eventually, but it was a hard struggle for a couple of years.

I questioned my parents endlessly. Why did you send me away? Why are we Freedomite Doukhobors? Why was there so much bombing and burning? Why are our people being put into prison? Why did we want to move to Russia? The answer was always the same: 'You'll find out when you grow up'. Well, I'm all grown up now, and I still don't have any of the answers. My dad and I would have debates, but none of the questions were ever answered straightforwardly. There were always things left unsaid, and I guessed it was up to me to figure things out for myself. Well, that was nothing new; I'd been doing it for the past few years anyhow.

There was a lot of tension in our household when I came home, and I understand many of the other children held in New Denver experienced the same thing. One man who was in the dorm as a boy says that when he got home he felt he was in the way of his brothers and sisters. I believe a lot of us felt that way.

Overall, my parents and sisters were very happy that I'd come home and that now we could have some sort of normal family life. Everyone tried hard, but I was unmanageable. I'd listen of course, but in the back of my mind I knew I was right and everyone else was wrong. I'd developed a feeling of superiority, though I'm not sure why, and for a short while the world revolved around me. Well, it did in my mind anyway. My grandmother Zebroff would say I'd become like an English (meaning non-Doukhobor) girl. I took that as a compliment, not a criticism. I just wanted to be like any normal kid. I knew my experience wasn't normal at all, so I did my best to fit in.

No one in my family grasped what I was going through. I tried to tell my parents, mostly my mom, about how I felt, but, kind as she was, I don't think she understood. My dad became even more strict as I grew older, and it wasn't until I was eighteen that our relationship became father-and-daughter once again. Up until that time he tried to rule, but I always thought he was far too unreasonable. He wanted me home by six p.m. I wasn't allowed to go for pop with the kids after school. I understand now that he was only trying to protect me because he was frightened of what I was capable of, and of what I might become, but I felt I'd escaped from one jail into another.

My mother never had harsh words to say about anyone or anything, even though I overheard some of the things others said to her. I asked her once why she didn't talk back, and she just said it was easier to ignore. Well, not in my world, because if you didn't speak up for yourself you'd be eaten alive. My attitude was one of aggression and retaliation. I wished sometimes I could be more like my mom, but that didn't happen. I was loud, aggressive, and always right - even when wrong. It was hard to let go of the upbringing of the previous few years. Mom and Dad succeeded in reining me in, though; I never got into any trouble with the law, or other authorities.

So, my relationship within the family after returning from New Denver was strained and strange. I knew they were my family, but I never felt I really belonged. It took me a long time to learn to trust again. Deep down I was still afraid of being sent away again. I have since learned to trust people. That is, until I'm done wrong; then it's over.

My children, too, paid a price for my years in New Denver. I sometimes treated them as if I were a major in the army. I thank the Lord that I'd catch myself doing it, and always gave them lots of love and hugs and kisses, and prayed they'd become good people. And they have.

* * *

As I write these lines that finally bring the account of this section of my life to a close, my daughter is preparing to deliver my first grandchild. I'm aware of standing at the threshold of a new phase of my existence, one defined by my relationship to a child whose happiness will depend to a large extent on the conduct of those of us privileged to be a part of her life. I pray I may be worthy of that sacred trust.

Our parents showed incredible courage, endurance and sacrifice in standing up for what they believed was right. I could never find fault with what they did, but I've questioned myself often as to how far I'd be willing to go for the sake of my beliefs.

May God bless all of our parents, for we know how much they loved us.

AFTERMATH

All Freedomite parents kept their word, and sent their children to local public schools the September following their release.

A large number of the Freedomite leadership were rounded up and jailed in the early sixties, which caused disruption to the movement as an organized force.

Plans to go to Russia were never accomplished.

Some who as children had been held in New Denver eventually requested that the provincial Ombudsman investigate their case. They claimed that as a result of their removal from their families they had suffered losses on a number of levels including loss of love, nurturing, guidance, their childhood, loss of privacy, dignity, self-respect, and individuality, and loss of civil liberties. In addition, some alleged physical and psychological maltreatment and unacceptable living conditions. The Ombudsman agreed to investigate.

April 1999: Forty years after the children's release the Ombudsman presented *Public Report No. 38 - Righting the Wrong: The Confinement of the Sons of Freedom Doukhobor Children*. The report concluded that their complaints were substantiated, and contained five recommendations. These were that the Attorney General on behalf of the provincial government:

1. Provide a clear acknowledgement that the government was wrong in the manner in which it apprehended and confined the children of the Sons of Freedom Doukhobors in the New Denver institution.
2. Provide the complainants with as full and adequate an explanation as would be reasonable and appropriate, given the passage of time, for why, as children, they were apprehended and confined in New Denver.
3. Make an unconditional, clear and public apology to the complain-

ants on behalf of the government, in the Legislative Assembly, for the means by which they were apprehended and for their confinement in New Denver. The essential elements of the apology were to include:

- a full and comprehensive explanation of why the children were institutionalized and detained in New Denver;
- an acknowledgement by government that the children were, by being institutionalized in New Denver, treated unfairly and unjustly both as a group and as individuals, and that harm resulted;
- acknowledgement that the harm was not intended and that the government expressed regret for the harm done; and
- a clear statement that the government would offer reparation for the harm done.

4. Consult with the complainants as a collective to determine the means by which they wanted to be heard, and the appropriate form of compensation. The consultation would:

- instruct government as to the manner by which compensation would be provided and designed for both individuals and the group;
- enable the complainants to construct the way in which compensation and support should be dealt with, to enable them to make choices and to heal; and
- be designed in such a way as to avoid any third party that is neither a complainant nor part of the group of complainants nor part of government being responsible for the design of the form of redress.

5. Refer the Report to the Commanding Officer "E" Division and urge him to consider the role of the RCMP in the matter and the appropriate action to take.

November 2000: The provincial government invited all former New Denver residents to a meeting to discuss the issues raised in the Ombudsman's Report. Following the meeting the Deputy Attorney General sent a letter to the former New Denver residents inviting them to identify how the government could provide support for projects that might serve as a proper legacy for the community.

April 2001: Fifty-five former residents of the New Denver dormitory filed an action in the Supreme Court against the government of British Columbia, alleging that they were systematically maltreated, humiliated and degraded during their time in New Denver. They specifically claimed that they had been:

f. hunted and arrested by police officers;

g. confined in a prison environment and regime;

h. denied all proper access to their families; the one hour meeting with family on the first and third Sunday of each month was, rather than comforting, extremely hurtful, humiliating and degrading as the visits were conducted with the children on the inside of the chain link perimeter fence and their families on the outside, with RCMP police guards present;

i. punished by having their visiting rights with family cancelled;

j. forbidden to practice their religion or use their mother tongue, Russian;

k. physically abused including excessive strapping and beatings;

l. sexually abused including denial of all privacy including being forced to change, toilet and shower in full view of the other children and the staff; some of the Plaintiffs were sexually assaulted by staff and older children; all of the Plaintiffs were forced to live in this state of sexual degradation and exploitation;

m. denied proper food, accommodation, health care and education;

n. forced labour;

o. denied any and all cultural rights; the Defendant belittled and denigrated the Doukhobor community, religion, language, values and customs; vegetarians were forced to eat meat; pacifists were forced to put on boxing gloves and fight; the confinement and the regime were designed by the Defendant to drive the Plaintiffs away from their family and community.

March 2002: The Ombudsman presented *Righting the Wrong: a Progress Report*, to inform the public of steps the government had taken to address the five recommendations contained in the original Report. The Progress Report reads, in part:

"...Recommendation #1: This recommendation has not been implemented. Government has not provided a clear acknowledgement that it was wrong in the manner in which it apprehended and confined the children of the Sons of Freedom Doukhobors in the New Denver institution.

Recommendation #2: This recommendation has been partially implemented. Government has attempted to provide an explanation for why the children were apprehended and confined. Government has provided an historical background to Sons of Freedom Doukhobor complainants in order to put the issues into context.

Recommendation #3: This recommendation has been partially implemented. Government has not made an unconditional, clear and public apology to the former New Denver residents in the Legislative Assembly. Having said this, elements of this recommendation have been addressed. In a November 22, 2000 letter written to former residents of New Denver, the Deputy Attorney General expressed regret for "what happened to you and your families".

Recommendation #4: This recommendation has been partially implemented. A number of meetings have been held to address this recommendation. Government has commenced a process of consultation with former residents of New Denver. While expectations regarding the outcome of these consultations undoubtedly differ among the parties, I am hopeful that ongoing consultations will eventually produce a mutually satisfactory outcome. Government has heard proposals from former New Denver residents for legacies in the form of commemorative art, an oral history project, and curriculum development. I encourage government and the former New Denver residents to continue to work toward a mutually agreeable resolution that properly embodies the spirit of this recommendation.

Recommendation #5: This recommendation has been fully implemented. A copy of *Righting the Wrong* was provided to the Commanding Officer RCMP "E" Division."

The Progress Report concluded: "While the response by government to date does not fully address the recommendations in Public Report No. 38, I am pleased with the efforts undertaken by government officials to explore creative means of addressing the outstanding recommendations. I remain optimistic that this ongoing process will lead to the full implementation of all of the outstanding recommendations contained in *Righting the Wrong*. I intend to continue to monitor and report publicly on the progress of the Ombudsman's recommendations."

April 2002: A pre-trial hearing in the Supreme Court determined that since some forty-two years had passed between the children's release from New Denver in 1959 and the filing of the action in 2001 their claim would normally be barred by British Columbia's *Limitations Act*. However, since a claim based on 'misconduct of a sexual nature', is not governed by any limitation period, the Court considered whether there was enough evidence to sustain such a charge in this case.

The claim of sexual misconduct rested on the complaint of one of the fifty-five complainants, that: (a) the dormitories at New Denver were cramped and overcrowded, allowing no privacy for the children; (b) he was required to dress and undress in the presence of his peers and occasionally in the presence of staff members; (c) the showering, bathing, and toileting facilities were communal and there were no doors on the toilets; and (d) older boys teased him about the size of his genitals.

The judge decided that there was no evidence that the dormitory conditions at New Denver were any different from those at most summer camps, or that the showering facilities were any different from those in most school gymnasiums or public pools. "I understand the distress that [the complainant] experienced at New Denver. However, I am unable to conclude that the physical conditions at New Denver, the resultant deprivation of privacy and the opportunity that provided for him to be teased by his peers, constitutes misconduct of a sexual nature." The case was accordingly dismissed.

September 2004: A complaint was filed with the BC Human Rights Tribunal on behalf of the 'New Denver Survivors Collective' alleging that the government had contravened the *Human Rights Code* by erecting a monument at a place of 'human suffering' in New Denver, BC. The Survivors Collective said that they had urged the Ministry for four years preceding the filing of the complaint not to erect a monument because this would discriminate against their ancestry.

"For us New Denver Survivors to accept a memorializing symbol is to dishonour our forefathers who gave their lives for this principle and passed on to us this same principle of honouring only the Living Spirit within each individual. The Unity Committee of Canada and the United States will shun our small group as traitors to the basic principles of our culture."

October 2004: BC Attorney General Geoff Plant issued a Statement of Regret in the legislature to Sons of Freedom Doukhobor children who were removed from their parents in the 1950s to attend residential school in New Denver.

"... We recognize that as children, you were caught in this conflict through no fault of your own. So on behalf of the government of British Columbia, I extend my sincere, complete and deep regret for the pain and suffering you experienced during the prolonged separation from your families.

"We recognize and regret that you were deprived of the day-to-day contact with your parents and the love and support of your families. We recognize and we regret the anguish that this must have caused. We will continue to offer counselling to former residents and your relatives including your siblings, your offspring and your spouses who wish to access this service. And we hope that this acknowledgement will enable you to work with us toward continued reconciliation and healing..."

January 2005: Attorney General Geoff Plant announced that due to vigorous opposition from the New Denver Survivors Collective a commemorative site in New Denver on which over ten thousand dollars had already been spent would not be going ahead as planned.

March 2008: The complaint to the BC Human Rights Tribunal was amended to include a claim of discrimination as a result of the government's alleged failure to implement the recommendations in the Ombudsman's Report. The allegations included:

- The Ministry had refused to provide the Survivors with an unconditional, clear and public apology for the means by which they were apprehended and for their confinement in New Denver; this refusal, and the manner in which the Ministry acknowledged the confinement of the Survivors, had the effect of minimizing the government's wrongdoing and of suggesting that their mistreatment was justified or excusable;
- The Ministry had failed to fully disclose to the Survivors why they had been incarcerated in New Denver, despite having access to historical records, documents and archives which would have provided such an explanation;
- The Ministry had failed to provide, or to engage in meaningful consultations about, the appropriate form of compensation; the Ministry ought to have known that the decision to construct a park and erect a monument on the New Denver site was hurtful, unacceptable and

demeaning to the Survivors, and yet despite the Survivors' rejection of the memorial the Ministry continued with its plans to construct it;

- The Ministry had treated the Survivors differently compared to others who had been subjected to historical wrongs perpetrated by the government, and had cultivated the view that the Survivors were less worthy than others who had been subjected as children to maltreatment in public institutions;
- The Ministry's actions and inactions had exacerbated the Survivors' hurt, humiliation and suffering, and perpetuated the historical injustice to the Survivors as a result of their wrongful incarceration in New Denver in the 1950s.

The Survivors said the discrimination was ongoing and constituted a continuing contravention of the Code. They sought a range of remedies, including an order that the Ministry implement the recommendations in the Ombudsman's Report. The BC Human Rights Tribunal issued a preliminary ruling accepting the complaint.

January, 2012: The BC Human Rights Tribunal hearing began into alleged discrimination by the Attorney General and the Ministry responsible for Multiculturalism. The New Denver Survivors stated that the complaint was not directly related to their seizure, but rather to the government's inadequate response to the Ombudsman's Report recommending they receive an apology and compensation. In April, 2013 the Tribunal determined no such discrimination had taken place.

* * *

The Dorm

A knock on the door, two men stood there.
'We've come for Helen, where is she?'
Mama said, 'We've been waiting for you. She's right here, come in and see.
'Please, give us an hour or two for her family to say goodbye.
I'll wash and comb her long, long hair, and remind her gently not to cry.'
Grandparents, aunt, sisters gathered round, and amidst cries and tears,
Reminded me to be so brave... and not to have any fears.

The two strangers came back for me. Took my little suitcase, packed up tight.
'Get in the back seat, little girl. We're sorry, but we have to do things right.'
I crawled in and looked about - my family's saddened eyes.
I must be brave, I told myself. Miss you already, but I won't cry.
We travelled all night long it seemed, the road so long and winding.
I'd never been so car-sick before. Mother's image before me, reminding:
'Be patient, polite and speak nicely...' 'They're always right, even when wrong.'
'Listen, learn and adopt their ways.' 'At eight years old, you've got to be strong!'

We arrived in New Denver at dawn, the day was awakening fair.
The first thing the matron did, took me inside and cut off my hair.
I cried and begged her not to... She wouldn't listen to me.
Proceeded with her course of action. 'THIS is the way things are gonna be!'
Dad told me to call the matrons 'Auntie' - A mistake right from the start.
The other kids thought me an outsider. That's where I stayed... Apart.
The English language, I spoke, and able to read and write quite well,
Convinced the kids that I was there, sent directly from HELL.
I tried to tell them they were wrong. None would listen to me,

Until one day this scrawny kid took me aside and said 'Hello,' to me.
'Tell me about yourself, Helen, and who you really are.'
I spent a long time talking and telling, I convinced her, became a star.
I could translate what we heard. Or, what on paper was written
To be scrawl, deciphered as on who the matron next was hitting.
Life became much easier then. I had friends I knew
No matter what happened next, beside me they would stick like glue.

Our parents, brothers and sisters visited now and then, it seems,
On a Sunday, twice a month, for one hour - Felt like some sort of dream.
They'd bring us food and clothing, to distinguish from the rest.
For we all wore the same issue, which was a far cry from the best.
We were also issued a number - They called me eighty-five -
Sewn onto every stitch of clothing, including assorted socks and gloves.
The dorms were neat and tidy, kept so clean by us in pain.
If the coin didn't bounce up high, the beds torn apart, and start again.
The floors so very shiny, took three of us to wield the mop.
Two to push, and one to steer... By day's end, we were ready to drop.
Guards outside the dormitory to see no one escapes at night.
Lights flooding the area totally... An inescapable nightmare of fright.

During visiting days, before us stand many RCMP, are they fully armed?
What sort of thing is happening here? Who can these young children harm?
If or when we didn't behave just right, our visiting privileges taken away.
Then, we wait an extra two weeks, to see those we love and for whom we pray.
When my sisters came to see me, I'd be edgy the whole time and want to
Shout....
Don't want them inside, with me. What if they wouldn't let them out?
For then, because I'm the oldest of three, I'd be responsible for them, too.
I can hardly look after myself. What then, Lord, what would I do?

We attended regular school. I certainly impressed the teachers.
For who could believe a dummy like me could understand their preaching.
I gathered certificates and awards, for work well done by me.
'Mama taught me right,' I said. 'Open your eyes, and see.'

Helen Chernoff Freeman

Grandpa Zebroff came to see me the first day I was there.
He stood beside the road we trod, not daring to come near.
I saw him standing all alone, I rushed and hugged him tight
Assured him I was really fine, learning and doing things right.

The matrons never gave up... 'No Russian to be spoken here!
You WILL be punished, so severely!' Filling us always full of FEAR.
One day my rubber overshoes fell off the spot '85' that was mine.
The matron swore she'd strap me... I got out of that one fine.
When we went to dinner - She sat by the window and drawled -
I flung myself on my stomach and up the stairs I crawled.
She didn't see me, I knew. The promised strap I never got.
Relief spilled out, all over me. Thank God, she really forgot!
She was such a mean one, the strap she administered coldly,
I'd just stare at her, my pulse racing, but I'd face the situation boldly.
Walk out of the office smiling, while on my wrists, blood starting
To come to the surface, in bubbles, the tears in my eyes... Smarting.
My friends, standing and waiting. 'How was it, bad?' They would ask.
'Oh (&**&%*), it hurts like HELL,' and back would come the mask.
We tried to be brave as can be, we the little children in chains,
Suffering for something we didn't understand, a lifetime won't erase the pains.

A gymnasium, built right on the grounds, for us to use.
The instructor, a mighty man, gave us nothing but physical abuse.
I have a gift for talking, no matter what is said.
He cut me short one day by throwing a basketball at my head.
He knocked me right off my feet. I just got up and stared
At him, my defences up. I'm the only one who cared.
Stars were sparkling in my mind. Felt kind of good not to hear
Him, yelling at me to smarten up. 'No talking - And no tears!'
One cold winter morning I woke up so sick. The mumps I developed, so
Cruel.
The matron did not believe me, and sent me off to school.
Another day, at supper time the food they served, NOT FAIR...
Looked like old, dead oranges floating in dishwater and bits of hair.

By this time I was smarter than ever in my life before.
Put the slop into plastic, then the pocket... Not a drop fell on the floor.
I was one of the lucky ones - The matron thought I'd eaten.
I could go out and play, those who did not eat
Sent to their beds, some were beaten.

We had a laundry on the site, Japanese people worked there too.
Along with some other kind people helped us children make it through.
The Japanese people were kind to us, we never expected them to be.
Perhaps they were remembering themselves how it felt to be FREE.

Parcels from home, laden with goodies, inspected first by them, so that
They could pick out what they wanted. Leave the rest for us, the Brats.
Letters too were always censored. What could an eight-year-old say
That would jeopardize their operation as it ran from day to day?

There were a couple of girls among us that knew no fear.
The matrons did not scare them at all, no matter what they hear.
A girl fixed one matron GOOD as she raced to wash the floor.
The matron said 'Hurry!' The girl put the mop in matron's face and asked 'MORE?'
For this, she got THE punishment. 'No visiting days for you,' matron said.
By now it didn't matter, the girl told her to drop dead.

We wanted to do away with a matron. The best way, we thought, use the door
That opens to the outside, against which we'd prop a polisher for the floor.
We never went through with it. 'We aren't criminals,' we said.
'We'll use no physical violence, play mental games instead.'
Things kept disappearing she thought she'd put away.
Her mind was playing games on her. 'She's on top of things, you say?'

Summers were for swimming. Winters for skating around.
The rapport we children had with each other, never again found.
An example I'm going to mention, is someone sitting in a tree.
Throwing apples to another, when questioned, said, 'What apples? Who, me?'

We even had entertainment, brave ones us three,
Putting on a show, picking on the boys, charging everyone an entrance fee.
To come and see this marvel, unrehearsed lines,
Everyone enjoyed it to the fullest, all commenting, 'Fine!' 'Fine!'
We had collected five dollars, a staggering sum, then.
Our older, wiser manager, took it, and then promptly spent.

Visiting days in winter, blankets draped over a fence seven feet high,
The winds and snow not halting until it was time to say goodbye.
Farewell kisses through a chain-link fence wasn't easy to do.
Warm lips would stick to cold metal, as if on it were glue.
We'd watch our parents walking away, and wish we could go too.
Instead, back to the dorms, shed silent tears, feeling so sad, lonely and blue.
Remember, we are just little children. WHAT is going on???
Why are we locked up like this? We did not do any wrong.
I guess it was for religion, those who believed in it so strong.
Parents... Children... Lives torn apart. Tell me, was it right or wrong?????

HCF

APPENDIX A

BC Ministry of the Attorney General

October 4th, 2004

STATEMENT OF REGRET TO SONS OF
FREEDOM DOUKHOBOR CHILDREN

As read by Attorney General Geoff Plant:

I rise in the House with the honour of paying tribute to special guests joining us today: [...] representatives of a special group of British Columbians, known as the New Denver Sons of Freedom Doukhobor Children.

I would like to take a few moments to talk about a sad chapter in BC history. The Provincial Ombudsman brought this chapter to the attention of government and the public in her 1999 report, *Righting the Wrong: The Confinement of the Sons of Freedom Doukhobor Children.* This report details the events that occurred some fifty years ago when 104 Sons of Freedom Doukhobor children were removed from their parents who were arrested during a protest in the West Kootenays. In 1953, some 104 children were taken by bus to New Denver where those of school age were kept in a residential care facility and those who were not of school age were returned to their families.

Over the next six years - from 1953 to 1959 - the government enforced a policy of mandatory school attendance and approximately 200 children were placed in the New Denver institution during this period. Many Sons of Freedom parents, determined not to surrender their children, hid them from the police. Initially, the children went to school in the institution, but eventually they were integrated into the local public school in New Denver.

No doubt the New Denver experience affected these children and their families in profound ways. In many cases these children were kept from their parents for extraordinary periods of time. Some children were not allowed to return home during the summer or at Christmas because of uncertainty that their parents would return them to New Denver.

This was not an easy story to hear nor is it an easy story to tell. I commend all those who came forward after all these years to talk about what must be extremely personal and painful memories. Many of these people, we have since come to learn, have buried their past and they even felt it necessary to hide their Sons of Freedom background and their association with New Denver from their friends, their neighbours and their employers.

The challenge that we, as government today, face in understanding what happened half a century ago is not as simple as one might expect. What we do know is that these were frightening times for the residents of the Kootenay and Boundary regions of British Columbia.

Bombings and burnings had been occurring throughout this part of the province for over three decades. Fear and anger had escalated among both the Doukhobor and non-Doukhobor communities. And to this end, the government of the day was under tremendous pressure to end the violence.

Mr. Speaker, we can't fully understand or explain the motives of a government of fifty years ago. We can, though, recognize the circumstances under which these events occurred and acknowledge how things might be done differently if we were to do them today.

I would like to thank those who had the courage to come forward to remind British Columbians about this history. Many of us were unaware or had forgotten about the conflicting values and the political turmoil that involved the government and these communities over half a century ago and in particular, too many of us were unaware, that you as innocent children were taken from your homes and your communities.

We recognize that as children, you were caught in this conflict through no fault of your own. So on behalf of the Government of British Columbia, I extend my sincere, complete and deep regret for the pain and suffering you experienced during the prolonged separation from your families.

We recognize and regret that you were deprived of the day-to-day contact with your parents and the love and support of your families. We recognize and we regret the anguish that this must have caused. We will continue to offer counselling to former residents and your relatives including your siblings, your offspring and your spouses who wish to access this service. And we hope that this acknowledgement will enable you to work with us toward continued reconciliation and healing.

Thank you, Mr. Speaker.

APPENDIX B

My Letter to the Attorney General

November 1, 2004
Attorney General

Dear Sir,

I am a New Denver Survivor. I was held at the Dorm from December 1955 until August 1959. My years spent there, can only be described as a terror-filled living HELL. I've spoken often in the past, and still do, of my years at the Dorm and have come to terms with myself, my beloved Parents John and Mary, the RCMP, the so called caregivers and the Government. I have forgiven where it was due, but I shall NEVER FORGET those sorrow filled years.

Counselling/Healing has been a part of my path for over 30 years. I appreciate the Healing Services being offered by the Government for the last year or so. I truly hope this service will continue for at least a few more years. I am taking advantage of this program, as are many others who are prepared to help THEMSELVES move forward with their lives.

I am definitely in favor of the Historic Site under construction in New Denver. The single, very important issue (in my humble opinion) about this site is AWARENESS. The statues of Mother and Child are an incredible work of art that captures the essence of what was. Sculpted by a fellow survivor, there is an energy emanating from this work, and it certainly is not romanticizing anything, let alone the plight of the children who resided at the Dorm. The viewer will sense a loss of childhood, and a great deal of hurt, pain, sorrow and yearning. An emptiness surrounds the Mother and Child, yet the viewer will also see a faint glimmer of hope for the future.

If one person who visits the Site comprehends what happened to the Freedomite Children, and then steps in and stops the abuse of ONE CHILD, no matter the circumstances, my years spent at the Dorm were worth every single minute.

I am extremely upset by the few people who are very verbal and claim to represent a huge majority of Survivors, yet seemingly have absolutely no respect for any opinions other than their own.

I did not participate in the lawsuit, push for a public inquiry, or demand an apology in the legislature. Yet, I honoured and respected those who did, for I believe we have all chosen our own life's path.

We all have the right to make our own choices. I choose to put the past behind me. I choose to continue in my healing and spiritual growth. I choose to look towards a future filled with understanding, peace, serenity and harmony with all.

I choose to accept, on my behalf, the statement of regret and acknowledgement of wrongdoings that you offered in the Legislature on October 4, 2004.

I choose to say, Thank You, Geoff, for it took courage to stand before the people of British Columbia to offer regrets for wrongdoings that happened some fifty years ago.

May peace surround you,

Sincerely,

Helen Chernoff Freeman

APPENDIX C

Attorney General's Reply to My Letter

21 November 2004

VICTORIA

Dear Helen Clewortt Freeman,

I am most grateful for – and was very moved by – your letter of November 1, and the directness of your approach to these very difficult chapters of your life and our history as a province. Thank you for giving me an opportunity to learn from your own experience.

Yours faithfully,

Geoff Plant —

APPENDIX D

Further Information

For the full text of the British Columbia Ombudsman's report:
British Columbia. Office of the Ombudsman. *Righting the Wrong: the Confinement of the Sons of Freedom Doukhobor Children* (Public Report No. 38, April 1999, to the Legislative Assembly of British Columbia). ISBN 0-7726-3898-5
For the full text of the British Columbia Ombudsman's follow-up report:
British Columbia. Office of the Ombudsman. *Righting the wrong: A Progress Report* (Public Report no. 43, March 2002, to the Legislative Assembly of British Columbia) Follow up report to: *Righting the wrong: the confinement of the Sons of Freedom Doukhobor Children*. Cf. P. ISBN 0-7726-4710-0
Available online at: www.ombudsman.bc.
For the full text of the British Columbia Supreme Court decision: Citation: **Arishenkoff v. British Columbia 2002 BCSC 488** Date: 2002 04 04 Docket: S011925 Registry: Vancouver. The Honourable Madam Justice P.A. Kirkpatrick
For the full text of the British Columbia Human Rights Tribunal decision: Indexed as: Swetlishoff v. B.C. (Ministry of Attorney General) (No. 2), 2013 BCHRT 106. Date Issued: April 26, 2013. File: 2103. Tribunal Member: Enid Marion

About the Author

Helen Chernoff was born into a Freedomite Doukhobor family in Oliver, British Columbia in 1947. Her early childhood was spent in Grand Forks, B.C. Shortly after Helen's eighth birthday she was removed from her home by police and taken to New Denver, B.C. There she was forced to live in a residential dormitory with other children of Freedomite parents. They were made to attend the local public school as part of a government policy of forced assimilation. Her experiences there provide the material for her first memoir, 'Girl #85 – A Doukhobor Childhood'.

Released from the Dormitory in August 1959, Helen attended public school in Grand Forks until 1962. Then, with her parents, grandmother and siblings, Helen joined the Freedomite Trek which began in the Kootenays region of British Columbia and headed for Mountain Prison in Agassiz, B.C. The Trek was to protest the incarceration of Freedomites on charges of domestic terrorism. Helen arrived in Agassiz in 1963 along with about twelve hundred others. The Doukhobors camped in a gravel pit a short distance from the prison. The camp remained until 1972, when the last of the prisoners were released. At that time, with the exception of a few families, the Doukhobors moved back to the Kootenays.

Helen stayed in Agassiz and married. Son Chris was born in 1970 and daughter Nicole in 1973. The marriage ended in 1984. Helen married Gerry Freeman in 1988. They both worked for Highland Helicopters in Agassiz until 1993, when Helen left to work at Park Place Restaurant, which they had purchased together. Gerry's untimely passing in 1999 was mourned by many people as he was the very popular Mayor of Agassiz.

With best friend Kathleen Makortoff, whom she first met while held as a child in New Denver, Helen appeared on 'In The Company of Women' for CBC and was featured in a documentary for W television entitled 'Daughters of Freedom'. Both productions were about Freedomite Doukhobors.

Today Helen shares her life in Agassiz with her partner Jerry. Her children Chris (Tiffany), Nicole (Derreck), and precious Grandbaby Aubrie live nearby.